FRANKLIN COMMUNITY LIBRARY
10055 FRANKLIN HIGH ROAD
ELK GROVE, CA 95758

D0116506

new WOK cooking

Also by Rosa Ross

365 Ways to Cook Chinese
Beyond Bok Choy: A Cook's Guide to Asian Vegetables
Chinese Healing Foods (with Suzanne LeVert)

new WOK cooking

EASY, HEALTHY, ONE-POT MEALS

rosa ross

CLARKSON POTTER/PUBLISHERS
NEW YORK

Published by Clarkson Potter/Publishers, New York, New York.
Member of the Crown Publishing Group.

Random House, Inc. New York, Toronto, London, Sydney, Auckland
www.randomhouse.com

CLARKSON N. POTTER is a trademark and POTTER and colophon are registered trademarks of Random House, Inc.

Printed in the United States of America

Design by Maggie Hinders

Library of Congress Cataloging-in-Publication Data
Ross, Rosa.
    New wok cooking : easy, healthy, one-pot meals / by Rosa Ross.
    1. Wok cookery. I. Title.
TX840.W65 R67 2000
641.5951—dc21   99-049909

ISBN 0-609-60418-X

10 9 8 7 6 5 4 3 2

First Edition

For Clara Ross Napolitano,
that she too will love to cook.

Acknowledgments

Writing may be a solitary occupation, but writing a cookbook cannot be. Without the participation of many, *New Wok Cooking* could not have been written.

Elise Goodman, my agent, believed in this book and made great efforts to place it. Pam Krauss, my editor, helped me shape the concept. Chloe Smith, Maggie Hinders, Carter Shaw, Liana Faughnan, and everyone else at Clarkson Potter gave able assistance. Thanks also to my friends and students, who talked, tasted, and tested: Clayton Cooke, Paul Grimes, Jonathan Leff, Sabine Renard, Cara Morris, Tracey Aberman, and Donna Adams. And, as always, appreciation goes to my daughters, Sarah and Samantha, and the many friends who critiqued my efforts and helped me arrive at the recipes included here.

Contents

introduction

Ask a chef what one piece of cooking equipment he or she couldn't live without and you'll get a variety of answers; one might treasure her trusty mandoline, while another couldn't imagine cooking without his cherished copper bowls. For me, the hands-down winner is my carbon-steel wok, a slightly battered, perfectly seasoned specimen that I've been using on a daily basis for more than a decade. In this one pan, I have deep-fried, steamed, poached, braised, boiled, seared, simmered, and, of course, stir-fried more meals than I can count. It's probably the least expensive pan in my kitchen and without a doubt the one most often used. I can't imagine cooking—not only Asian cuisine but all the cooking I do—without it. ● I spent my early childhood in Hong Kong in a household where cooking was done by servants, behind closed doors. As was customary in homes in British

Hong Kong, ours was a sleek Western kitchen dominated by an imposing, gleaming white gas stove for cooking the multicultural dishes that we ate. I am sure, however, that Cook had his trusted wok at the ready for preparing myriad Western dishes as well as Chinese cooking. I know that whenever my family went camping in the New Territories or hiking in the hills of Kowloon, we always brought along a wok to cook our meals over an improvised wood fire "stove." We would dig a trench about 5 inches deep, and set the wok on two stones or bricks. With only a few twigs and some brushwood, we produced enough heat to cook. The only other cooking vessel we brought along was a deep pot, usually aluminum, for cooking rice. The wok worked for all our meals—bacon and eggs sunny-side up for breakfast, and stir-fries, stews, and soups for everything else. For us, it was second nature to cook all kinds of meals with the wok.

In my modern American kitchen, I must admit, more than a few kinds of pots and pans have made their way into my cabinets, yet I still turn to the wok for a variety of techniques. In talking to my cooking students as well as friends, I have discovered that most of them use their woks simply for stir-frying. But as the family camping trips taught me at a young age, and as I've proved repeatedly since then, the wok is the ideal implement for cooking anything and everything. It has the perfect shape—little changed since ancient times—for the efficient use of fuel and conducting heat. It is capacious but not unwieldy—a large wok can hold a whole chicken, duck, or fish with ease. Its contours make it possible to arrange food, such as cut-up chicken or meat, in a single layer to allow for braising and an even distribution of flavor. The unique shape of the wok permits it to heat up more quickly and evenly than a flat-bottomed pot or skillet, and the reduction of broths and sauces requires less time. With the addition of a rack and cover, the wok can be converted to a steamer, or even a smoker, and the sloping sides allow it to accommodate large bamboo steamers of varying sizes. Less liquid is required for poaching and deep-frying than with a regular pot, and food can be pushed up the sides to drain. And then there is my favorite plus: When cooking dishes sequentially, only *one* pan needs to be washed! A basic carbon-steel wok is extremely inexpensive, and even if you go for a fancy stainless-steel or coated wok, the investment is still small when compared with the cost of a standard French *batterie de cuisine*.

Because in most cooks' minds the wok is still associated with Asian fare, and because these are the flavors I know and love best, I've built the recipes in this book on a pantry of Asian ingredients. But this is far from a traditional Chinese cookbook. If you follow my guidelines, you'll be able to build your menu as Asians do. By adding to the basic rice or noodles a different cooking technique for each "taste" or dish, you can keep your everyday menus varied. The braised, poached, steamed, and one-pot dishes that you will read about here often lend themselves to reheating, and many can be made ahead and refrigerated or even frozen. The recipes I offer will allow you to consistently make exciting and unusual dishes. I hope this book will expand both your world of wok techniques and the dishes, ingredients, and tastes of your cooking repertoire.

New Wok Cooking opens with a chapter on basic broths, the foundation of great flavor in every cuisine. Most of the soups in chapter 2 can serve as one-dish meals, and because so many of them incorporate ingredients that are best stirred and mixed in, the shape of the wok again makes this the best pan to use. I can never decide which method I prefer for wok cooking: braising, steaming, or poaching. I only know that I rarely think of using any pan other than my wok when I choose to prepare a dish using one of these methods, so naturally there are chapters based on these techniques. I have included chapters on stir-frying and deep-frying, techniques synonymous with wok cooking. Smoking becomes an everyday technique when you use a wok, and you will find that my chapter on tea-smoking makes it even simpler and easier to enjoy smoked food. The condiments chapter covers sauces, dressings, and oils that complement wok-cooked food and includes my own favorite recipes, many of which make great gifts; and finally the sweets chapter echoes the cooking methods central to this book.

To introduce you to the wide world of wok cooking, I have included a section on stocking a wok pantry (pages 6–12). You will find many staple items available at the supermarket; health-food stores are also good sources. Others may require a trip to an Asian market; if that is impossible, there are now many excellent mail-order resources, and some allow you to shop on-line. See page 209 for a listing of sources.

Rice is to Asian food as bread is to the West, but because this staple is not cooked in a wok, I've placed the rice recipes at the end of "Your New Wok Cooking Pantry" (pages 13–14).

a word on woks

I must confess to owning many kinds of woks, but if I had to choose only one, a well-tempered carbon-steel wok with a stainless or aluminum lid would be my first choice. You will notice that I have recommended a specific wok for each recipe. This does not mean that you must run out and buy a wok *batterie*; rather, if available, the wok specified would be the ideal kind to use. A good wok can be purchased anywhere for a nominal amount, so there is no need to spend a fortune on equipment. For those of us intent on splurging on kitchen stuff, or where price is no object, there are many types of woks that can cost a bit of money—porcelain lined, stainless steel, coated aluminum, and even copper. Whichever type you choose, make certain it has a domed cover, preferably made of rustproof aluminum or stainless steel.

Carbon Steel—Carbon steel is the type most recommended for stir-frying, and it also works well for deep-frying and tea-smoking. It is light, conducts heat well, and maintains high temperatures; the least expensive wok can cost as little as $5 in Asian markets. A carbon-steel wok must be tempered before use. Tempering can be done by simply placing a clean, oiled wok over a medium flame and heating it until the oil is absorbed. Do this over a period of approximately one hour, oiling the wok three or four times with an oil-soaked paper towel. A carbon-steel wok comes from the manufacturer coated with grease, which must be washed off with detergent. Tempering closes the metal molecules, thus making the wok nonstick. If improperly washed or used with liquids, as when poaching, steaming, or braising, this wok must be retempered to restore its nonstick qualities. A carbon-steel wok must be thoroughly dried or it will rust. The easiest way to dry the wok is to place it in a warm oven or on a stovetop over low heat for a few minutes.

Stainless Steel—This type is great for poaching, steaming, braising, and deep-frying because the stainless steel need never be tempered. It conducts heat well and retains heat, cooling down more slowly than a carbon-steel wok. Some brands, such as All-Clad, are also good for stir-frying, but they tend to discolor when used over dry heat, as in tea-smoking.

Coated Aluminum (not to be confused with nonstick)—Excellent for poaching, steaming, braising, deep-frying, and tea-smoking, though not an ideal choice for stir-frying, as food tends to stick.

Electric Woks: stainless, nonstick, and coated—Few stir-frying authorities have a kind word for electric woks, for although they will heat to over 400°F., they cool rapidly when even a small amount of food is added, making them a poor choice for stir-frying. However, they are useful in that they provide a separate heat source away from the range top. They are great for steaming and work well as poaching and braising pans.

Finally, here are a few tips to make wok cooking easier. If you do not have a high-heat stove, don't fret. To compensate, use a thin carbon-steel wok, which will conduct heat faster than other pans. Stir-frying works best when you preheat your wok until the oil begins to smoke, and then add the ingredients. This ensures the quick cooking necessary with the constant tossing that is an intrinsic part of stir-frying, and the dish acquires a smoky flavor, called *wok hey* in Cantonese, an attribute highly valued. Stir-fry your meat, poultry, or seafood in batches so that the food sears and seals quickly without losing its juices. To prevent your wok from wobbling, choose a flat-bottomed wok, or turn the burner ring around the gas fire upside down so it cradles the wok; you can also sit your wok on the ring that comes with most woks. For those who have to stir-fry on an electric stove, the best thing to do is to have one burner on high and one on low and move the wok back and forth when a quick change in heat is required.

A SHORT LIST OF SPECIAL EQUIPMENT

Generally, regular pots, skillets, and casseroles will work fine for the recipes in this book; however, a few pieces of inexpensive equipment will make things easier for you. Everything is available in most Asian markets and specialty kitchen stores.

- 14-inch or larger carbon-steel wok with domed aluminum or stainless lid
- 10- to 12-inch bamboo steamer baskets (at least 2) with bamboo lids
- Round metal racks that will fit into the wok to create a rack for steaming and smoking
- Wire mesh strainer
- Long bamboo chopsticks
- Long-handled spatula

- Chinese-style ladle
- Flat plates (8 or 9 inches round) and bowls (5 to 6 inches round) with a rim or lip about 2 inches high for wet steaming
- Small metal or glass Pyrex bowls for preparing sauces
- Spice grinder (I use an inexpensive electric coffee grinder reserved for this purpose)

your new wok cooking pantry

I am often asked how to make food taste authentically Chinese—or Thai, Malaysian, Vietnamese, or Japanese. The answer is to have a pantry of basic ingredients that typify those cuisines. In this section, I list the assortment of ingredients that will enable you to prepare both the traditional dishes and the modern interpretations you'll find in this book. My recipes incorporate flavors from China, Japan, Southeast Asian countries, and even India. Once you become comfortable and familiar with these wonderfully flavorful and exciting ingredients, I hope you will use them to come up with your own Asian-inspired dishes.

Begin your pantry with basic Chinese ingredients, the foundation of most Asian kitchens. Many of these ingredients may already be familiar to you and are readily available in supermarkets and groceries. Once you have your basic Chinese pantry, you will need to add only a few items to obtain the characteristic flavors of other Asian cuisines. With your wok pantry established, you will be able to cook any of the recipes in this book without special trips to Asian groceries or specialty food markets. The majority of ingredients are dry, preserved, and shelf-stable and will keep for a very long time. (A few sauces should be refrigerated after opening, particularly if you will not be using them up quickly.)

Just as the mirepoix, a mix of aromatic vegetables—onions, carrots, and celery—is the first step in defining the flavors of the French and Italian kitchens, ginger, scallions, and garlic are key in Chinese cooking. Some variation of these three seasoning vegetables, with the addition of a few characteristic ingredients, defines the flavors of the Thai, Vietnamese, Indonesian, Korean, Japanese, Malaysian, and Indian kitchens.

But before we begin, here is my note on the universal seasoning, without which all food would be tasteless—salt. Sadly, salt has acquired a bad reputation of late and even many with no health limitations have embraced the practice of cooking without any salt. It is vital that we use salt *when we are cooking, not at the table*. I find that kosher salt is the most flavorful and has the advantage of being available in every supermarket. This is the salt I prefer and the salt that is used in all my recipes. Quantities specified may vary slightly if you use a finer-grained salt, so adjust seasoning as necessary.

The other ingredient that is in all of our kitchens is water. Don't ever be afraid to add and use water in your recipes. This is particularly important when you are doing long, slow cooking. During that time, the liquid may evaporate too much and the dish become dry. If you add broth or another flavored liquid after an hour or two of cooking, the flavors will become unbalanced, whereas adding water is only putting back what has been lost in the cooking. Don't worry about diluting the dish too much and losing some of the taste.

While the following list might seem long, read through it carefully, then take pencil to paper and make a list of staples you wish to keep. All the spices and dried items are shelf-stable and keep indefinitely. Do as I do, and set aside a shelf in your refrigerator for bottled sauces, just as you would for mustard, mayonnaise, ketchup, and specialty oils.

THE CHINESE PANTRY

Aromatic Vegetables and Key Flavors: Ginger, scallions, garlic, and soy sauce.

Asian Sesame Oil: A rich, dark brown, nutty oil made from roasted white sesame seeds. Used as a "perfume," it is generally added as a last step in cooking a dish, for it provides both a sheen and flavor. This oil is not intended to be used as a cooking oil. It is highly perishable and, once it is opened, turns rancid quickly at room temperature, especially in hot weather. I recommend that you refrigerate sesame oil unless it will be used up within a month or so.

Bamboo Shoots: These tender shoots have a pleasant mild flavor and crunch. Canned shoots are widely available. Fresh shoots may be found at times in Asian markets; they must be peeled and parboiled before use in recipes.

Bean Curd: Commonly called tofu. In this book, the names are used interchangeably. Tofu is very high in protein and is regarded as the "meat" of Asia. Usually sold fresh and very perishable. The type—silken, soft, firm, extra firm—depends on the amount of water re-tained when the bean curd is made, a process that involves setting the soybean milk with a coagulant such as gypsum. Tofu may be frozen for 24 to 48 hours to change its texture; frozen tofu makes a good meat substitute in vegetarian dishes.

Black Sesame Oil: Similar in flavor to regular sesame oil, it is made from toasted black sesame seeds.

Cassia Bark: Very similar to cinnamon but has a stronger flavor. Available in dried chunks that look just like tree bark.

Chilies, Dried: Come whole or in flakes. Used to add spice to dishes. Popular in Szechwan and Hunan regional dishes. Cayenne may be substituted if necessary.

Chinese Dried Black Mushrooms (Dried Black Winter Mushrooms, Dried Shiitake Mushrooms): These delicious fungi may be used interchangeably and are available in many grades. Use less expensive grades as an ingredient for adding to dishes; use meatier, more expensive grades for stuffing and in dishes where mushrooms are the main ingredient.

Cilantro: Always used fresh in Chinese cooking, often as a garnish. In the Thai and Vietnamese kitchens, the whole plant, including the roots, is used. Do not substitute seeds—they have a different flavor.

Dried Shrimp: A strong-smelling, strongly flavored ingredient that comes in many sizes and grades, dried shrimp cannot be used as a substitute for fresh shrimp. Also very popular in Thai cooking, where it is often powdered and mixed with chili flakes to be used as a garnish and sprinkled over food.

Dried Tree Ears: Dried fungus that grows on tree bark; sometimes sold fresh. Two varieties are commonly available: one is very small, wrinkled, and black; the larger gray-and-black type has a tougher texture. Used to add texture to dishes, this fungus has no flavor. Recent medical research indicates that tree ears have properties that benefit the heart.

Fermented Black Beans: These fermented black soybeans are usually sold salted, sometimes with the addition of orange peel. They should be rinsed and lightly mashed before they are added to dishes. They keep for months in a tightly closed container on the shelf. Also sold in sauce form ready to use; the sauce should be refrigerated after opening.

Five-Spice Powder: A highly aromatic flavoring made up of cassia bark (or cinnamon), cloves, fennel, Szechwan pepper, and star anise.

Glutinous Rice: Also called sweet or sticky rice, this short-grain rice has a very high starch content and is therefore sticky. Used for stuffings, pottage, and desserts.

Hoisin Sauce: A sweet sauce made from soybeans and spices—which I like to call Chinese ketchup because it has the same appeal as a table sauce. It adds a sweet, slightly spicy element to many kinds of dishes and burnishes nicely when used on grilled foods.

Hot Chili Sauce: A spicy table sauce or ingredient made of ground red chilies and spices usually bound with a thickener. Some versions contain garlic or soybeans. Not as hot as the pure Thai chili sauces or Indonesian chili sauce (sambal oelek).

Noodles:

FRESH WHEAT FLOUR NOODLES *(MEIN)*: Come in different shapes and sizes; there are also many dried varieties.

RICE NOODLES *(FUN)*: Made with rice flour, these noodles are sold both fresh and dried. Vermicelli and linguine shapes, always dried, are called *mei fun* and are used in stir-fried noodle dishes and soups. These puff up dramatically when tossed in hot oil and make a great garnish. Fresh rice noodles, also sold in broad sheets, are called *ho fun* and may be eaten without further cooking.

MUNG BEAN NOODLES *(FUN SI)*: Made with mung bean flour, these noodles are also called bean threads, cellophane noodles, or glass noodles; they turn transparent when cooked. They sometimes contain potato starch.

Oyster Sauce: A thick, brown sauce made from the essence of oysters and spices and used as a cooking ingredient, served directly from the bottle or thinned with a little soy.

Rice Vinegars: The mild vinegars made from rice have much less acidity than other wine vinegars.

WHITE RICE VINEGAR: The most common type, this vinegar is used sweetened to flavor sushi rice and to make simple, quick pickles.

RED RICE VINEGAR: Pale red or pink in color, it is popular in Chinese cooking for use at the table, often with shreds of ginger.

BLACK VINEGAR: Made in Chekiang and widely appreciated for its characteristic and unmistakable flavor, this is the Chinese parallel to Italian balsamic vinegar. Used in sauces to give a special flavor; also used at the table with ginger shreds. A great dipping sauce for dumplings.

Seaweed:

HAIR SEAWEED: A popular and expensive ingredient in Buddhist vegetarian dishes.

LAVER: An ingredient valued for its protein and iodine, but not as prevalent as nori is in the Japanese kitchen.

AGAR AGAR: Also called *kanten,* this seaweed is sold in powder form and used as a gelatin; it will gel at room temperature. Agar agar also comes in thin strands, like white, transparent noodles. In this form, it is soaked in cold water and used as an ingredient in salads. Never soak in hot water, which will melt it.

Sesame Paste: A butter made from toasted sesame seeds. It usually contains no salt and is not homogenized, so it will separate. Keep refrigerated after opening.

Sesame Seeds: There are two varieties, black and white. Both have the same flavor, so make your choice based on aesthetics.

Shrimp Paste: Sold in jars or in blocks, shrimp paste is not to be confused with dried shrimp; nor are the two ingredients interchangeable. The Chinese and Filipinos use a milder version than do Southeast Asians; and the Indonesians like a dried block (*trasi*), which is stronger. Both versions should be toasted or fried before use; a jarred version comes already fried. Highly aromatic, with a strong, pungent flavor and aroma.

Soy Sauces:

THIN SOY SAUCE: Defined by its light color and higher salt content, it is used at the table and in cooking when the light or white color of the food is to be maintained, as it will not darken the dish.

DARK SOY SAUCE: Also called black or double black, it is usually less salty, as it is made dark by the addition of caramel for coloring. The key ingredient in Chinese "red" cooking, it gives dishes a dark color as well as a soy flavor.

Star Anise: A star-shaped, anise-flavored seedpod.

Szechwan Peppers: Also called *fagara,* these peppercorns are very fragrant and aromatic but not spicy. May be used directly from the package, but are best dry-toasted to bring out their aroma before use.

Tapioca Flour: Used in dumpling doughs to give the dough translucence when cooked.

Water Chestnuts: Mildly flavored corms with a crunchy bite that appear fresh in Asian markets year-round. Canned water chestnuts cannot compare in flavor with the fresh and should be used only for their texture and convenience. Fresh water chestnuts are crunchy, very sweet, and well worth the effort to peel. Choose hard fresh water chestnuts; they turn powdery as they age.

Wheat Starch: The flour that remains after the gluten has been removed. Used in dumpling doughs.

Yellow Bean Sauce: Also called bean sauce, yellow bean paste, and bean paste, this thick paste is made from preserved soybeans and spices. Some varieties are completely smooth; others contain coarse bits of bean. Bean sauce must be cooked.

THE JAPANESE PANTRY
Aromatic Vegetables and Key Flavors: Ginger, scallions, dashi, and miso. Less use of garlic than in the Chinese kitchen.

Chili Peppers with Sesame, Nori, and Orange Peel: Also called *nanami togarashi*. Used as a condiment and flavoring.

Mirin: Sweetened Japanese rice wine used in cooking. Great for caramelizing grilled dishes, especially fish that cooks quickly.

Miso: A paste made from soybeans, grains, salt, water, and culture, which is available in many varieties, differentiated by grain content and length of aging time. For general use, miso falls into two categories:

WHITE MISO: Light in color, with a gentle, sweet flavor.

DARK MISO: Deep red brown, with a deeper, nuttier flavor.

Noodles: In addition to somen, the Chinese-style wheat noodles, there are:

UDON: Thick wheat flour noodles.

SOBA: Buckwheat noodles.

Nori: Dried laver, which comes toasted (with a purplish tinge) and untoasted. Use toasted nori to save a step. Has a rough-textured side and a smooth-textured side. Used as a wrapper in sushi; can also be crumbled and used as an ingredient.

Panko: Coating crumbs (like bread crumbs) made from wheat starch. Stays crisp even when cold, and it absorbs very little grease.

Pickled Ginger:

PINK GINGER (AMAZU SHOGA): Paper-thin slices of pink ginger pickled in white rice vinegar and sugar. Used as a palate freshener with sushi, as an ingredient, and as a pickle.

RED GINGER (BENI SHOGA): Fine shreds of bright red pickled ginger; saltier than pink ginger. Used as an ingredient.

Sake: Rice wine, which comes in many grades and varieties. Used in the kitchen to cook with; also a great drink, served warm or ice cold.

Sansho: Japanese pepper with a special flavor.

Shiso: Resembling a very large flat parsley leaf, this jagged leaf has a licoricelike flavor and comes in two varieties, green and purple. Used as a flavoring herb in cooking and in sushi. Can be used in pickles, salads, and egg dishes.

Umeboshi Plums: Very tart pickled plums. Used as an ingredient in sweet and savory dishes.

Wasabi: Japanese horseradish, with a strong, hot, mustardlike flavor. Comes in a fine powder that is mixed with a little water to make a stiff paste. Can be served as a condiment with sushi and can be used as an ingredient, much as dry mustard is.

THE SOUTHEAST ASIAN PANTRY: THAILAND, VIETNAM, MALAYASIA, AND INDONESIA

Aromatic Vegetables and Key Flavors: Shallots, galangal, lemongrass, lime leaves, cilantro, chili peppers, and fish sauce. More use of fresh herbs than in the Chinese kitchen.

Banana Leaves: An attractive dark green, these leaves are used as wrappers. They are inedible and impart no flavor. Readily available frozen in ethnic markets, including Spanish markets; very rarely available fresh. The frozen leaves should be defrosted and rinsed in warm water before use.

Coconut Milk: Unsweetened "milk" made by steeping boiling water in the grated flesh of the coconut (not the juice of the coconut, usually only a tablespoon or two of slightly cloudy liquid). Thick coconut milk is extracted from the first two cups of steeped water; thin milk, from the next two cups. Coconut cream is the rich layer that rises to the top of thick coconut milk that has been allowed to stand for a while; two cups of milk will yield about two inches of cream. Canned, unsweetened coconut milk, now available in most supermarkets, is the most convenient form to use, and the quality is very good. There are also powdered and frozen forms. For those who are concerned about the fat content of coconut milk, A Taste of Thai's Lite Coconut Milk with 70 percent less fat makes a good substitute for any recipe in this book calling for coconut milk.

Fish Sauce: Salty sauce made with fermented fish. Used instead of soy sauce to produce the characteristic flavor of the cuisines of Southeast Asia, notably Thailand (nam pla), Vietnam (nuoc mam), and Malaysia.

Galangal: An aromatic rhizome of the ginger family, without the spiciness of ginger.

Kaffir Lime Leaves: The Kaffir lime, which has a rough green skin, is seldom available and not very aromatic. The lime leaves may be found both fresh and frozen and have a strong, perfumed, citrus flavor. Do not keep frozen leaves too long, as they lose their aroma in time. When the leaves turn black, they should be discarded. Either fresh or frozen can be used in recipes. If you purchase a large amount of fresh leaves, freeze them, for this is the best way to keep them.

Lemongrass: Citronella. A tropical grass with a lemony citrus flavor. Usually only the tender white stalk is used. It does not cook away but remains coarse, so it should be left in pieces and removed or sliced very, very thinly.

Rice Noodles and Vermicelli: Sticks and linguine-shaped types are available. Reconstitute by soaking in hot water and cooking very briefly. The linguine shape is popular in Thailand and Vietnam, but it is not used in the Chinese kitchen.

Rice Paper: Paper-thin sheets of dried rice paper are available in circles and quarters of various sizes. Shelf-stable. Reconstitute by dipping in warm water and letting stand for a few minutes to soften. Ready to eat as is, but can be steamed or deep-fried to a crispy finish.

Tamarind: Sour-tasting pulp of the seedpod of the tamarind tree, usually purchased in a block. Tamarind pulp must be soaked in hot water before use. Tamarind water and pulp, with seeds removed, is used in recipes.

Thai Chili Sauce, or Sambal Oelek: Very hot and spicy chili sauce made with ground red chilies, salt, and vinegar.

THE INDIAN AND SRI LANKAN PANTRY

Aromatic Vegetables and Key Flavors: Onions, shallots, garlic, ghee (clarified butter), aromatic spices, curry leaves, turmeric, and chilies for spice.

Curry: Various blendings of spices, which are aromatic and pungent and vary in degree of spiciness. The spices may be raw or toasted (characteristic of Sri Lanka) and almost always contain cardamom and curry leaves, which are best used dry. Curry also refers to the long, slow, braising or stewing cooking method, in other words, a stew.

THE KOREAN PANTRY

Aromatic Vegetables and Key Flavors: Lots of garlic, scallions, ginger, sesame, chilies, and, of course, kimchee, the spicy pickled cabbage.

Even with the best-stocked pantry, we sometimes find ourselves out of something. Here are some ideas that work in a pinch. Use the substitutions in the same quantities as the original ingredients.

Ingredient	Substitute
PLUM WINE	Soak 1 or 2 prunes in Madeira for 30 minutes, then drain and use the flavored wine.
YELLOW BEAN SAUCE	Miso. Although they are not identical, this works.
SHRIMP PASTE, FISH SAUCE, AND ANCHOVY PASTE	All can stand in for one another.
WHEAT NOODLES	Any pasta, fresh or dried.
PALM SUGAR	Brown sugar, packed.
CASSIA BARK	Cinnamon stick.
THAI CHILIES	Jalapeños.
SWEET SOY (ketjap manis)	Dark soy sauce sweetened with brown sugar and flavored with 1 or 2 star anise pods.
BROTHS	Low-sodium chicken, vegetable, or fish broths. Also clam juice mixed with chicken stock or water makes a good substitute for fish stock.
SESAME PASTE	Chunky peanut butter.

RICE TO SERVE WITH WOK-COOK DISHES

Although this is a book on wok cooking, it would not be complete without a few recipes for steamed rice to pair with our wok dishes. Whether the rice comes out dry with separated grains or sticky depends on the length of the grains of rice. Long-grain rice contains less starch and will be drier. For sushi or Japanese-style rice, use a medium-grain rice, and for creamy dishes, such as puddings and risottos, use a short-grain rice.

Basic Steamed Rice

This recipe uses the traditional Chinese method for measuring the water and is foolproof, whether you are cooking 1 cup of rice or 10 pounds. You need only be concerned that the pot will hold the rice, which should double in volume once it is cooked. We will use a measure of rice for the sake of the recipe.

MAKES ABOUT 8 CUPS; SERVES 4 TO 6

3 cups rice, long grain or medium grain, or quantity needed

Place the rice in a saucepan or pot that will hold twice the amount of the raw rice. Rinse the rice in cold running water several times until the water runs almost clear, then drain.

Add cold water to cover the rice by about 1 inch, measured from the top of the rice to the first joint of your middle finger; or add enough water to cover your hand when laid flat over the top of the rice.

Place the pot over high heat, bring to a boil, and cook, uncovered, at high heat until the water is almost completely absorbed and small "chimneys" form on the surface of the rice. At this point the grains of rice will be hard and raw at the center.

Immediately reduce the heat to low, cover the pot, and steam the rice for about 10 minutes, or until each grain is completely cooked through. Hold over low heat until ready to serve. (The rice will not burn, but a hard crust will form and brown the longer it sits over low heat. This crust, called *fan chui,* which means crisp rice in Cantonese, is a popular home-style treat. Usually, cold tea is poured over the *fan chui* to loosen it, and it is eaten with the tea as a choice treat.)

Perfumed Rice

For curries and savory stews, I often add sweet spices to the steamed rice for an extra bit of flavor. The nuttiness of basmati rice blends nicely with the spices.

SERVES 4 TO 6

3 cups basmati rice
1 bay leaf
6 whole cloves

Combine the rice, bay leaf, and cloves in a saucepan. Add water to cover by 1 inch and cook as directed for Basic Steamed Rice (page 13).

Spiced Coconut Rice

Rice steamed in coconut milk instead of water is a popular dish to serve with curries in Southeast Asia. This version is a little different: Perfumed spices are added to the cooking liquid.

SERVES 4 TO 6

2 cups unsweetened coconut milk
2 cups water
2 cups jasmine rice
1 teaspoon ground cumin
1$\frac{1}{2}$ teaspoons ground coriander
$\frac{1}{2}$ teaspoon ground cloves
1 tablespoon salt
$\frac{1}{2}$ teaspoon freshly ground white pepper

In a saucepan, combine the coconut milk and water. Add the rice and stir in the cumin, coriander, cloves, salt, and pepper. Bring to a simmer, cover tightly, and cook for about 20 minutes, until the rice is soft. Fluff with a fork and steam over low heat for another 5 minutes.

1

basic
broths

In all fine cooking, but particularly in Asian cooking, broths play an important role in the kitchen. They are the backbone of soups and an essential element of tasty braises, stews, and sauces. Without a flavorful broth, dishes will be bland and uninteresting. And though the quality of canned and frozen stocks has improved somewhat, they are a poor second to homemade stocks. ● In my cooking classes, I find that students who are new to cooking have trouble grasping the advantages of making their own basic broths and stocks. Their main objection is always the length of time it takes, and my standard response is that the actual prep time is next to nothing. Once a broth is started, there is no need to stand in the kitchen hovering over the simmering stock; it will take care of itself very nicely and at the end of two hours or so, you will have the foundation for making many dishes with tremendous depth of flavor. Although most of the broths in this chapter do require a long, slow simmer, there are several that require much less cooking time. Dashi (page 24) is ready in only 10 minutes, while Fish and Shrimp Broth (page 24) and Tamarind Broth (page 18) can both be made in as little as 30 minutes.

Having invested time in making a large pot of broth, you will, of course, want to store it properly. All the broths that follow may be made ahead and refrigerated, properly covered, for 3 to 5 days. Freeze them for several months. If you are short on room, be aware that stocks can be reduced simply by letting them simmer until some of the liquid has evaporated. Being impatient, I like to use my wok to reduce stocks because the larger surface area allows for faster evaporation, and I can cut the cooking time by more than half. Of course, the flavors will be concentrated, but you can always adjust for this by adding water when you are ready to use the broths. An interesting exercise that pays off if you are really tight on space is to reduce a large stockpot of broth to such a degree that you end up with what is essentially a bouillon cube from which tiny bits can be cut off and reconstituted. You don't have to go this far, but I know that once you get into the habit of making and having broths on hand in your own kitchen, you will be amazed at how easily and quickly you can prepare delicious soups and many other dishes.

vegetarian broths

Basic Vegetable Broth

You will be surprised at the sweet flavorful broth that results from just a few simple vegetables. When I lived in Italy, I learned to make this broth to use as a base for my daughter's baby formula because it is so full of vitamins and nutrients. The first time I wanted to serve this with fish as an elegant first course for a catered dinner, my partner, Paul Grimes, who is totally French in his training and outlook, refused to believe we could get any flavor from just a handful of vegetables and water. The result bowled him over. Though there is nothing Asian in the basic ingredients, the slow simmer that produces a clear broth is a very Asian technique.

MAKES ABOUT 6 CUPS

```
8 carrots
4 celery stalks
1 medium onion
6 romaine lettuce leaves
12 cups cold water
Salt, for serving
```

In a large stainless-steel or coated-aluminum wok or stockpot, combine the carrots, celery, onion, romaine leaves, and water. Bring to a boil, reduce the heat, and simmer uncovered for about 3 hours, until the broth is sweet and flavorful. The broth will be reduced by half. Strain and discard the vegetables. Salt lightly to serve or store as suggested on page 16.

Simple Coconut Broth

This is a good base for the many coconut soups found in Asian cooking, and you can also use it for braises and curries. I have devised this broth as a way to reduce the fat in coconut milk while retaining the flavor. Low-fat coconut milk, available in most supermarkets, can be used in place of regular coconut milk.

MAKES 4 CUPS

1 15-ounce can coconut milk, regular or low-fat
1 cup nonfat milk
2 cups Basic Vegetable Broth (page 17)
6 Kaffir lime leaves, slivered
2 fresh or dried hot chilies
1 teaspoon salt

In a stainless-steel or coated-aluminum wok or saucepan, combine the coconut milk, nonfat milk, vegetable broth, lime leaves, hot chilies, and salt. Bring to a simmer over low heat and cook uncovered for about 30 minutes, until the broth is flavorful. *Do not let it boil,* or the broth will curdle. Strain and discard the vegetables. Use immediately or store as suggested on page 16.

Tamarind Broth

The tart taste of tamarind appears in many popular Southeast Asian soups and stews. With this broth as a soup base, you can add just one or two shrimp, bits of cooked meat, or pieces of fish and a few sprigs of vegetables and mint for a quick light lunch.

MAKES ABOUT 8 CUPS

2 ounces tamarind pulp
1 tablespoon dried shrimp
1 small onion, quartered
10 cups cold water
1 tablespoon thin soy sauce
1 whole scallion
2 small plum tomatoes
1 teaspoon grated lemon zest

In a wok or saucepan, combine the tamarind pulp, dried shrimp, onion, and water. Bring to a boil, reduce the heat, and simmer uncovered for 5 minutes. Add the soy, scallion, plum tomatoes, and lemon zest. Return to a simmer and continue cooking for another 30 minutes, or until the broth is flavorful. Strain through cheesecloth and discard the solids. Store as suggested on page 16.

Mushroom Broth

To add another layer of flavor to the woodsy taste of fresh wild mushrooms, I have included dried black Chinese mushrooms in this recipe. The result is so good that you could reduce the broth, thicken it with arrowroot, add a pat of butter, and use it as a sauce. For those not concerned about calories, heavy cream may be used for thickening in place of the arrowroot.

MAKES 4 CUPS

2 ounces dried Chinese black mushrooms
10 ounces white button mushrooms
¼ pound fresh shiitake mushrooms
1 tablespoon minced shallots
2 tablespoons light olive oil
4 cups cold water

Soak the dried mushrooms in a bowl of warm water for 15 to 20 minutes, until soft. Drain, reserving the soaking liquid. Remove and discard the stems. Clean the fresh mushrooms with a damp paper towel. Remove and discard the shiitake stems. Slice the button mushrooms and shiitake mushrooms.

In a stainless-steel or coated-aluminum wok, sauté the shallots in the olive oil for about 30 seconds, until soft. Add the sliced fresh mushrooms and sauté briefly. Add the water, the reserved mushroom soaking liquid, and the dried black mushrooms. Bring to a boil, reduce the heat, and simmer for 45 minutes, until the broth is flavorful. Strain the broth and discard the mushrooms, or mince for use in a sauce or another dish.

Ginger Broth

The ginger flavor of this broth makes it ideal for serving with wontons or dumplings that have rich fillings, such as pork, scallop mousse, or other seafood. When I add wontons to this broth, I like to prepare it in a wok because the larger surface allows the wontons to float freely as they cook. You can leave the slivered ginger in the soup or strain it out, as you prefer.

SERVES 6 TO 8

1½ ounces fresh ginger
4 cups Basic Chicken Broth (page 22) or Basic Vegetable Broth (page 17)

Peel the ginger and slice very thinly. Cut into fine slivers.

In a small wok or saucepan, combine the broth and the ginger. Bring to a simmer, uncovered, and cook gently for 10 to 15 minutes, until the broth is flavored with ginger. Serve as a clear soup or as suggested above.

Lemongrass Kaffir Lime Broth

The flavor of lemongrass dissipates quickly, so I recommend that you make this broth on the day you wish to use it. For a less perfumed flavor, leave out the Kaffir lime leaves.

MAKES 4 CUPS

4 to 6 stalks lemongrass
6 fresh or frozen Kaffir lime leaves
4 cups Basic Vegetable Broth (page 17)

Discard any coarse outer leaves from the lemongrass. If the green tops are fresh, add them to the broth for more flavor; otherwise, trim off and discard any dry, brown parts. Cut the lemongrass stalks into 3-inch pieces. With the blunt edge of a cleaver, crush the white parts of the stalks. Stack the lime leaves and roll them up, cigarette-fashion, then cut crosswise into fine slivers.

In a saucepan, combine the broth, lemongrass, and lime leaves. Simmer for 20 to 25 minutes, until aromatic and flavored. Strain and discard the solids. Use the broth immediately.

poultry, meat, and seafood broths

Duck Broth

Use the carcass of a duck for this recipe, saving the choice breast and thigh-leg pieces for another use. There will be ample flavor extracted from what is left on the bones and from the bones themselves. You can use both cooked or uncooked duck bones here. Because the duck is rich tasting, I incorporate the French technique of adding some dry white wine for a bit of acidity.

MAKES 8 CUPS

2 whole ducks (each about 5 pounds)
1 bay leaf
4 sprigs of fresh thyme
1 teaspoon black peppercorns
1 tablespoon Szechwan peppercorns
1 onion, quartered
4 carrots
1 celery stalk
4 slices fresh ginger (each about the size of a quarter)
1½ cups dry white wine

Remove the duck breasts and thigh-leg joints and reserve for another use. Remove all visible fat from the carcasses. (The fat can be rendered for use in cooking or discarded.) Tie the bay leaf, thyme, black peppercorns, and Szechwan peppercorns in cheesecloth.

In a large stockpot, place the duck carcasses, onion, carrots, celery, bag of herbs and spices, ginger, and wine. Cover with cold water. Bring to a simmer and cook uncovered over low heat for 4 hours, or until the broth is flavorful.

Cool for 30 minutes, then strain the broth. Discard the duck parts and vegetables. Cool the broth completely and degrease. If time permits, to degrease most effectively, refrigerate the broth until the fat hardens and then lift off all the fat and discard. If not using immediately, store as suggested on page 16.

Basic Chicken Broth

This quick, simple chicken broth is the basic cooking stock for many of the soups and dishes in this book. It can be reduced for easy storage. The broth will become cloudy if boiled rapidly, but of course the taste will not be affected. For use in soups, however, Asians prefer a broth that is clear and flavorful. Try to find an old hen, sometimes labeled soup fowl; it makes the most flavorful broth.

MAKES ABOUT 10 CUPS

1 chicken or soup fowl (about 4 pounds) or an equal weight of
    chicken parts
12 cups cold water
2 whole scallions
2 slices fresh ginger (each about the size of a quarter)

In a large stockpot, place the chicken in water to cover. Bring the stock to a boil over medium heat, then immediately reduce the heat to a low simmer, and cook for 10 minutes. With a slotted spoon, remove any scum that rises to the top; then add the scallions and ginger. Simmer for about 4 hours, until the broth is flavorful.

Cool and discard the chicken and the vegetables. Strain the broth through a fine sieve to remove all the solids. Cool and degrease completely. If not using immediately, refrigerate the broth, covered, for up to 5 days or freeze for up to 6 months.

Turkey Broth

Although this is not a traditional Asian recipe, I like the added dimension turkey imparts to a poultry broth. This is quite easy to make. If you wish, you can rinse out the cavity of your Thanksgiving turkey and use the carcass for this broth. For the variation, you can use pearled barley, but I, like most Asians, prefer the Scotch or pot barley, which has more fiber.

MAKES 8 CUPS

2 pounds turkey legs
1 carrot
1 onion, quartered
1 celery stalk
2 whole scallions
2 slices fresh ginger (each about the size of a quarter)
10 cups cold water

In a stainless-steel or coated-aluminum wok or stockpot, combine the turkey legs, carrot, onion, celery, scallions, and ginger with water to cover. Over high heat, bring to a boil, then reduce the heat and simmer uncovered for 2 to 3 hours, until the broth is flavorful. Strain and discard the solids.

Variation: For a hearty soup, add 1/2 cup barley and simmer for an additional 30 minutes. Season with salt and freshly ground black pepper, and serve.

Rich Meat Broth

The combination of meats in this recipe is very typical of Chinese cooking. The broth can be served by itself or used as a base for other soups or as an ingredient in various dishes. Brown the bones in a wok with a little oil, in the traditional manner.

MAKES ABOUT 10 TO 12 CUPS

2 medium yellow onions, unpeeled
2 carrots
2 celery stalks
2 tablespoons vegetable oil
1 pound beef with bones, such as short ribs or beef shank
1 pound pork with bones, such as spareribs, end-cut chops with
    bones, or fresh pork knuckle
2 pounds chicken parts, such as wings, backs, legs, thighs,
    and necks
3 slices fresh ginger (each about the size of a quarter)
3 whole scallions
16 to 18 cups cold water

Quarter the onions, peel the carrots, and cut the celery stalks into thirds. In a carbon-steel wok, heat the oil and brown the vegetables, tossing often. Remove to a deep stockpot. Add the beef with bones to the wok, a few pieces at a time, and brown, tossing often. Remove browned pieces to the stockpot. Repeat with the pork until all the meat is done. Deglaze the wok with water, scraping up all the brown bits, and add the drippings to the stockpot.

Add the chicken parts, ginger, scallions, and water to cover. Bring the stock to a boil, reduce the heat, and skim off the scum that rises to the top. Continue skimming for about 10 minutes. Cook over low heat, uncovered, for about 4 hours, until the broth is flavorful.

Strain and discard all the solids. Cool the broth and degrease completely. Or refrigerate overnight, then remove all the congealed fat. If not using immediately, store as suggested on page 16.

Dashi

Dashi is to Japanese cooking what basic chicken stock is to French cuisine. Dried black kelp, called *konbu* in Japanese, and shaved bonito flakes, also known as *katsuo bushi,* are used for this stock. Because they are dried, a supply can be kept on hand at all times. Surprisingly, these two simple ingredients produce an absolutely clear, flavorful broth with a nice smokiness. The kelp and bonito flakes can be reused; this less rich "secondary" dashi is the traditional base for miso soup.

MAKES ABOUT 6 CUPS

10- to 12-inch piece of dried black kelp *(konbu)*
6½ cups cold water
¾ cup shaved bonito flakes

In a large saucepan, combine the dried kelp with the water and place over high heat. As soon as the water comes to a boil, immediately remove the kelp. Remove the saucepan from the heat and immediately add the bonito flakes. Cover and let steep for 10 to 15 minutes, until the flakes sink to the bottom of the pan. Strain the broth through cheesecloth, and the clear dashi is ready for use. It can be stored in the refrigerator for up to three days.

Fish and Shrimp Broth

This is really a basic fish stock, with shrimp shells added for more flavor. The shells also clarify the broth. I recommend making this stock in a wok, which will easily hold the fish head and bones. Avoid fish that have too oily a flavor, such as bluefish or mackerel.

MAKES ABOUT 8 CUPS

2 pounds fish head and bones
8 to 10 cups water
2 whole scallions
2 slices fresh ginger (each about the size of a quarter)
Shells from 1 pound of shrimp

Place the fish head, bones, water, scallions, and ginger in a stainless-steel or coated-aluminum wok or large deep pot, and bring just to a simmer, uncovered, over low heat. *Do not boil.* Cook for 18 to 20 minutes, until the stock is flavorful. Add the shrimp shells and continue to simmer for another 5 to 10 minutes. Strain and discard the solids. If not using immediately, store as suggested on page 16.

2

soups

Soups are an intrinsic part of every Asian meal and they often serve as quick one-dish meals or snacks as well. There is nothing I like better for lunch than a large bowl of noodles floating in a tasty broth, topped with a slice or two of chicken, meat, seafood, or fish and a few sprigs of vegetables. Choose a wok to cook your noodle soup, and you will find that you can have a delicious meal in minutes. ● Cooking soup in a wok may at first seem a bit of a stretch. In fact, a wok has several distinct advantages over a saucepan or deeper stockpot when it comes to soup making. The wok is perfect for blending noodles into a broth; it allows more surface room for ravioli or soup dumplings to float freely to the top as they cook, thus preventing them from sticking to one another, and the wide shape of the wok makes cooking and mixing large chunks of fish or meat an effortless job. ● Although your everyday carbon-steel wok is perfectly fine for soups, the many "modern" woks available today are ideal, especially if you intend to let your soup stand for any length of time before serving. Stainless-steel woks, coated woks, and even electric woks are all excellent for cooking soups. You will find the wok's shape indispensable when preparing our chunky Thai-Style Chicken Soup with Rice (page 32), Green Papaya Amaranth Soup (page 28), and Curried Mussel Bisque (page 42). So, even if the idea of cooking soup in a wok seems unnatural at first, give it a try. I think you will be pleasantly surprised by this unusual way to use your wok.

soups with vegetables and tofu

Soupy Mushroom-Flavored Noodles

Although this is not strictly a soup, I have included it in this chapter because it makes a delightfully slurpy one-dish lunch. Stir-fry the mushrooms in a wok and then finish this richly flavored noodle dish in the same pot. The soup, mushrooms, and noodles are all comfortably accommodated by a wok, which allows you ample room to stir and mix without spilling bits onto the stovetop.

SERVES 2

4 ounces rice stick noodles
4 dried Chinese black mushrooms
4 ounces fresh shiitake mushrooms
4 ounces fresh white button mushrooms
1 tablespoon light olive oil
2 scallions (green and white parts), minced
1 tablespoon dry sherry
2 tablespoons soy sauce
1 cup Basic Vegetable Broth (page 17)
2 tablespoons minced fresh parsley
½ teaspoon freshly ground black pepper
Salt to taste

In a small bowl, soak the rice stick noodles in hot water for 20 minutes, until soft. In another bowl, soak the dried mushrooms in ½ cup warm water for 10 to 15 minutes, or until soft. Drain the mushrooms, reserving the soaking liquid, and slice them into shreds. With damp paper towels, clean the shiitake and white mushrooms. Discard the shiitake stems. Cut the shiitakes into shreds and slice the white mushrooms.

In a stainless-steel or coated-aluminum wok, heat the oil over medium heat and stir-fry the scallions, shiitakes, and white mushrooms for 1 minute. Add the shredded dried mushrooms, sherry, soy, mushroom soaking liquid, and vegetable broth. Bring to a simmer and cook for about 5 minutes, or until the mushrooms are tender. Drain the noodles and add to the mushroom mixture. Add the parsley and pepper, and cook for another 1 to 2 minutes, or until the noodles are warm. Season with salt to taste, and serve.

Green Papaya Amaranth Soup

When they first saw amaranth on field trips to Chinatown, my students thought they would only use the pretty green and red leaves for garnish. When they found that this vegetable could color soups and stews a lovely pink, amaranth became a favorite ingredient. This soup is not only delicious but pretty to look at, with chunks of green papaya, orange winter squash, and pale pork floating in the pink amaranth-colored broth. Served in soup bowls over mounds of rice, this makes a hearty main dish.

SERVES 8

2 teaspoons vegetable oil
1 tablespoon shrimp paste
2 pounds pork neck or rib bones
10 cups water
1 1-inch-square tamarind pulp soaked in warm water for at least
    10 minutes
2 small red chilies, fresh or dried
2 pounds pork butt
1 medium green papaya (about 1½ to 2 pounds)
1 small Hubbard squash (about 3 pounds) or 2 cups pumpkin chunks
1 medium white boiling potato
1 pound red amaranth
2 tablespoons fish sauce (*nuoc mam* or *nam pla*)
1 teaspoon freshly ground black pepper
2 tablespoons fresh lime juice

In a large stainless-steel or coated-aluminum wok, heat the oil and sauté the shrimp paste over medium heat. Add the pork bones and stir-fry for 2 to 3 minutes. Add the water, tamarind pulp, and chilies. Bring to a boil, reduce the heat, and simmer for 1 hour, skimming often during the first 10 minutes.

Meanwhile, cut the pork butt into 1-inch cubes. Peel and seed the papaya and squash. Cut into chunks. Peel the potato and cut into chunks. Wash the amaranth. Remove the stems and discard. Drain the leaves in a colander.

With tongs, remove the pork bones from the broth and discard them. Add the pork, papaya, squash, and potato. Cook for 30 to 40 minutes, until the meat and vegetables are tender. The soup may be prepared up to this point and held, or even refrigerated overnight. To finish the soup, add the amaranth, fish sauce, and black pepper. Cook for 5 minutes, until the amaranth wilts and the soup is tinted pink. Stir in the lime juice and serve.

Flat Rice Noodles
with Simmered Vegetables

The noodles called *ho fun* are sold ready-to-eat in Asian groceries. With a supply of them on hand, you can transform nearly any soup into a meal-in-a-bowl. You can substitute any kind of hearty noodle for the *ho fun,* such as udon, thick wheat noodles, or rice sticks. Because the *ho fun* are already cooked, take care not to overcook them when reheating. Green daikon is a variety of radish that looks like the white daikon but is tinged green. They are too sharp to be eaten raw, but sweeten when cooked.

SERVES 4

1 tablespoon vegetable oil
2 teaspoons minced peeled fresh ginger
1 garlic clove, minced
¼ cup dark soy sauce
2 tablespoons dry sherry
4 cups Basic Vegetable Broth (page 17)
1 pound winter squash, peeled and cut into chunks
2 carrots, peeled and sliced
1 small green daikon, peeled and cut into chunks
1 cup soybean sprouts or bean sprouts
4 scallions (green and white parts), cut into 2-inch pieces
½ pound flat rice noodles *(ho fun)*
Few drops of Asian sesame oil
Salt and freshly ground black pepper to taste

In a stainless-steel or coated-aluminum wok, heat the oil over medium heat. Add the ginger and garlic, and stir-fry until aromatic. Add the soy sauce, sherry, and 2 cups of the broth, and blend; then add the winter squash, carrots, and daikon. Bring to a simmer and cook for 20 minutes, or until the vegetables are tender. Add the soybean sprouts, scallions, and remaining stock, and cook for another 3 minutes. Add the noodles and cook just until they are heated through. Stir to blend. Drizzle with the sesame oil. Season to taste with salt and pepper, and serve.

Miso Soup

Everyday miso soup is usually prepared with secondary dashi, that is, broth made from "recycled" ingredients (see headnote, page 24). For a more elegant miso soup, substitute primary dashi, omit the tofu, and add bits of cooked meat, raw fish or seafood, and shredded vegetables, such as bamboo shoots, shiitake mushrooms, snow peas, or scallions.

MAKES 2 CUPS

2 cups dashi (page 24)
1 to 2 tablespoons white miso
¼ pound soft tofu, cut into ½-inch cubes
1 scallion (green part only), minced

Bring the dashi to a simmer. In a small bowl, whisk the white miso with ½ cup of dashi. Stir the miso mixture into the dashi in the pot. Add the tofu and scallion, and heat for a few more minutes before serving. Do not let the soup boil.

Soft Tofu in Spicy Lime Broth

Throughout Asia, soft or silken tofu cubes are often floated in clear soups. I thought serving the soft, delicate-flavored tofu squares in a spicy, gutsy broth would give a yin-yang contrast to this soup.

SERVES 4 TO 6

1 ounce bean threads
½ pound soft or silken tofu
4 small fresh hot red chilies or 2 jalapeño peppers
6 cups Basic Vegetable Broth (page 17)
2 tablespoons fish sauce (*nuoc mam* or *nam pla*)
6 Kaffir lime leaves
1 teaspoon freshly ground black pepper
Juice of 2 limes
Strips of lime zest, for garnish

In a bowl, soak the bean threads in warm water for about 15 minutes, or until soft. Drain and cut into 4-inch lengths, if desired. Cut the tofu into small cubes. Slice the chilies; do not remove the seeds if you want the broth to be really hot and spicy.

In a stainless-steel or coated-aluminum wok, combine the broth, fish sauce, chilies, lime leaves, and black pepper. Bring to a boil, reduce the heat, and simmer for 10 to 15 minutes, or until the broth is flavorful. Remove the lime leaves and discard them. Add the bean threads and tofu, then stir in the lime juice and heat for another 5 minutes. Garnish with the lime zest and serve.

soups with poultry and meat

Thai-Style Chicken Soup with Rice

The chicken in this recipe is cooked with the skin and bones intact, as is commonly done in Asia. I find that chicken pieces break up easily when turned too much during cooking, so I like to prepare this soup in a wok, which makes mixing easier and keeps the chicken from falling apart. The flavors develop even further as the soup sits, so prepare enough to serve it again the next day. This delicious one-pot meal makes an unusual Sunday-night supper. For a Western touch, serve it with a green salad.

SERVES 6 TO 8

1 tablespoon vegetable oil
1 medium onion, chopped
10 garlic cloves, crushed
1 tablespoon shrimp paste
1 teaspoon turmeric
3 cups Basic Chicken Broth (page 22)
2 cups coconut milk
1 tablespoon minced peeled fresh ginger
3 stalks lemongrass, cut into 2-inch pieces
1 tablespoon minced peeled galangal
5 Kaffir lime leaves
1 tablespoon fish sauce *(nuoc mam* or *nam pla)*
Juice of 2 limes
3 long hot chilies or 5 jalapeños, minced
½ teaspoon salt, or to taste
3 pounds chicken parts (breasts, thighs, and legs), with skin and
   bones in place

In a stainless-steel or coated-aluminum wok, heat the oil over medium-high heat. Add the onion and garlic, and stir-fry until wilted. Add the shrimp paste and turmeric, and cook, stirring, for 20 seconds, until aromatic. Be careful not to burn the turmeric.

Add the chicken broth, coconut milk, ginger, lemongrass, galangal, lime leaves, fish sauce, lime juice, chilies, and salt. Bring to a simmer and cook over low heat for 20 to 30 minutes, until the broth is flavorful. Remove the lime leaves and discard them. Add the chicken pieces and cook for 30 minutes, or until the chicken is done, turning gently a few times.

Ladle the chicken and soup over mounds of white rice, and serve.

Sliced Duck and Tamarind Soup

The citrus tang of tamarind balances the fatty richness of duck meat in this complexly flavored soup—a perfect dish for fall. Because the duck is seared in the wok, nearly all the fat is rendered and the skin is nicely browned, making it far less greasy than many other duck preparations.

SERVES 4

4 dried Chinese black mushrooms
2 boneless duck breast halves
4 cups Duck Broth (page 21)
1 1-inch-square tamarind pulp, soaked in ½ cup hot water for at
    least 10 minutes
2 1½-inch pieces of dried tangerine peel *(chenpi)*
1 tablespoon thin soy sauce
1 tablespoon dry sherry
1 teaspoon freshly ground black pepper
¼ cup snow peas, cut into fine slivers
¼ cup julienned carrot
¼ cup julienned daikon
¼ cup julienned scallion (green and white parts)
1 cup cooked soba noodles

Soak the mushrooms in ½ cup of hot water for about 20 minutes, or until softened. Drain, reserving the soaking liquid. Remove the stems and discard them. Slice the mushrooms into thin shreds and set aside. Score the skin on the duck breasts. Heat a carbon-steel wok until very hot. Add the duck breasts, skin-side down, and sear over medium-high heat. When the skin is brown and most of the fat has cooked off, turn the breasts and cook the other side for 8 to 10 minutes until done. (The meat will be rare.) Remove the duck breasts to paper towels to drain. Slice the breasts and keep them warm.

Pour off and discard the duck fat from the wok, and wipe off any excess fat with paper towels. In the wok, combine the duck broth, mushroom soaking liquid, tamarind pulp and water, and tangerine peel. Bring to a simmer and cook over low heat for 15 minutes. Remove the peel and discard. Add the soy, sherry, pepper, mushrooms, snow peas, carrot, and daikon, and simmer for 1 minute. Add the scallions, and return to a simmer for 30 seconds.

Divide the noodles among 4 bowls; top each portion with some of the sliced duck. Ladle the hot soup and vegetables over the duck and noodles, and serve immediately.

Velvet Chicken Dumplings in Lemongrass Broth

I use the classic Chinese way of preparing velvet chicken for this soup, but instead of poaching the quenelle-like dumplings in oil, I poach them gently in water. The delicate flavor of the lemongrass broth shines through in this recipe, but make only what you need—the lemongrass flavor dissipates very quickly. Also, you may substitute 4 cups of Lemongrass Kaffir Lime Broth (page 20) for the broth here. These dumplings are also delicious served with Hot Red Pepper Vinaigrette (page 183), and can be made a day or two in advance and refrigerated.

SERVES 4

For the Dumplings
6 ounces boneless, skinless chicken breast
2 slices peeled fresh ginger (each about the size of a quarter)
4 egg whites
2 tablespoons heavy cream (optional)
¼ cup minced chives
½ teaspoon salt
¼ teaspoon freshly ground black pepper

For the Broth
8 cups cold water
4 carrots
1 celery stalk
1 large onion
4 stalks lemongrass

1 cup pea sprouts or finely julienned scallion greens

Prepare the dumpling mixture: Trim all the fat and membranes from the chicken, and cut the meat into chunks. With the food processor running, drop in the ginger and mince finely. Add the chicken and process until you have a fine paste. Add the egg whites, one at a time, and process until well blended. Add the heavy cream if you're using it, and pulse to incorporate. Add the chives, salt, and pepper, and pulse to blend well. Remove to a small bowl and refrigerate for 30 minutes.

Fill a stainless-steel or coated-aluminum wok about half full with water. Bring water to a gentle simmer. With two wet spoons, form oval dumplings using about 1 tablespoon of the mixture for each. (You should have 16 to 18 dumplings.) Drop the dumplings into the simmering water. Do not let the water boil. The dumplings will rise to the surface as they cook. After all the dumplings have risen, simmer them for another 5 minutes to allow them to cook through. Remove the cooked dumplings with a slotted spoon and hold until ready to serve.

For the broth, place the water, carrots, celery, and onion in a stainless-steel or coated-aluminum wok. Remove the coarse outer leaves of the lemongrass. Crush the white part of the stalks and add to the pot. Bring to a boil and simmer over low heat for 2 hours, or until the broth has a nice sweet flavor. Remove the lemongrass with a slotted spoon and discard. Just before serving, blanch the pea sprouts in the broth, divide evenly, and mound in the middle of four soup plates. (If using scallion greens, do not blanch them.)

Arrange four dumplings per serving on the pea sprouts or scallion greens. Gently pour the broth over the dumplings and serve immediately.

Rich Beef Tea

This tonic soup is valued for its strengthening properties, and in Asia it is often given to underweight children or sick people with little appetite. Even though the broth is quite clear, its meaty taste makes it very satisfying as a light lunch if a few noodles and vegetables are added. Beef tea should be made in a water bath to slowly extract all the meat flavor. A glass or porcelain 9-inch casserole with a cover works well here.

MAKES 5 CUPS

1 flank steak (about 1 pound)
6 cups cold water
Salt to taste

Trim the flank steak and cut it in half lengthwise. Slice the steak crosswise in very thin strips. Place the meat and cold water in a deep casserole, cover, and stand the casserole in the wok. Fill the wok with enough water to come halfway up the sides of the casserole. Bring the water in the wok to a simmer, and steam for about 4 hours, until the soup is flavorful. Be sure to replenish the water in the wok during cooking. Strain the soup, discarding the beef. Season with salt and serve.

Coconut Beef and Noodle Soup

If your budget will allow it, use beef tenderloin for this soup; the ends of the tenderloin are perfect. Traditionally, the beef is cooked right in the soup, but I find that this makes the meat tough and its texture rough on the tongue (something that is undesirable in Asian cooking); so although this is an extra step, I like to stir-fry the beef first so that it remains tender and smooth.

SERVES 4

6 ounces beef tenderloin, sirloin, or top round
2 teaspoons cornstarch
2 teaspoons thin soy sauce
2 ounces bean thread noodles
3 teaspoons oil
1 tablespoon Madras curry powder
3 cups Rich Meat Broth (page 23)
1 cup coconut milk
2 teaspoons salt
6 to 8 snow peas, slivered
2 scallions (green and white parts), cut into 2-inch pieces
½ cup (loosely packed) cilantro sprigs

Cut the beef into slices about ¼ inch thick. In a small bowl, combine the cornstarch and soy sauce; add the beef and toss, coating well. In another bowl, soak the bean threads in warm water for about 15 minutes, or until soft and pliable.

In a carbon-steel wok, heat 2 teaspoons of the oil until very hot. Add the beef and stir-fry for 3 to 5 minutes, until seared. Remove to a plate. Heat the remaining teaspoon of oil in the wok and stir-fry the curry powder, being careful not to let it burn. Add the broth, coconut milk, and salt. Bring to a simmer over low heat and cook for 15 minutes; do not let the soup boil. Drain the bean threads and add them to the broth. Combine well, then add the snow peas, scallions, and beef. Mix well, ladle into bowls, and top with the cilantro.

Beef and Udon Noodles in Spicy Broth

Thick udon noodles have a delicious, satisfying chewiness that is lost when the noodles are overcooked. They are available fresh in Asian groceries and can be dropped directly into the soup. It is important to cook them evenly and quickly, which the wok, with its shallow wide shape, accomplishes like a charm. Hearty and tasty, this soup makes a perfect one-dish meal.

SERVES 2

4 ounces flank steak
2 teaspoons cornstarch
1 tablespoon plus 1 teaspoon dark soy sauce
Pinch of sugar
2 teaspoons oil
4 cups Rich Meat Broth (page 23)
1 tablespoon sake
2 teaspoons mirin
1 to 2 teaspoons chili paste or to taste
8 ounces fresh udon noodles
1 scallion (green and white parts), minced
2 teaspoons Asian sesame oil

Cut the flank steak into slices about 1/4 inch thick by 2 inches long. In a small bowl, combine the cornstarch, 2 teaspoons of the soy, and the sugar; mix well, then add the beef and toss to coat.

In a carbon-steel wok, heat the oil until just smoking. Add the beef and stir-fry for about 2 minutes, until just done but still pink in the center. Remove to a plate. Add the broth, the remaining soy, sake, mirin, and chili paste to the wok. Bring to a boil, reduce the heat, and simmer for 5 minutes. Add the udon noodles and cook for 5 to 8 minutes, or until the noodles are cooked through. Add the beef and stir to mix well. Sprinkle with the scallion, drizzle with the sesame oil, and serve.

Hairy Basil *(Mengluk)* with Noodles and Shrimp in Lemongrass Broth

This soup may seem similar to Shrimp and Rice Stick Noodle Soup (page 41), but it is the distinctive lemony taste of the basil that defines the broth. *Mengluk* is my favorite of the Thai basils, but it is very fragile and difficult to find. If you like to garden, it is easily grown and seeds are available from Shepherd's Garden Seeds. You can, however, substitute any other Thai basil. This is a perfect low-fat lunch, and if all diet food tasted like this, I wouldn't mind dieting every day. I know you will agree.

SERVES 2

4 ounces rice noodles
1 quart Lemongrass Kaffir Lime Broth (page 20)
2 slices galangal (each about the size of a dime)
½ cup *mengluk* basil leaves, torn, plus additional sprigs for
    garnish
1 tablespoon minced scallion (green and white parts)
1 tablespoon fish sauce *(nuoc mam or nam pla)*
½ pound medium shrimp, peeled and deveined
½ tablespoon lime juice

Soak the rice noodles in hot water for 20 minutes, until soft and opaque. Drain and set aside.

In a stainless-steel or coated-aluminum wok, bring the broth to a simmer. Add the galangal and simmer gently for 10 minutes; discard the galangal. Add the basil, scallion, fish sauce, and noodles, and stir gently to mix. Bring to a simmer and cook for 3 minutes. Add the shrimp and cook for another 3 minutes, until the shrimp turn pink. Add the lime juice, garnish with the sprigs of basil, and serve.

"Meatball" Soup with Soba

The "meatballs" in this soup are so delicious, you should consider making an extra batch to serve on the side. Try them simmered in a simple soy-based sauce—for a terrific main dish.

SERVES 6

1/3 pound shrimp, shelled and deveined
1/3 pound flounder fillets
1/3 pound lean pork
2 tablespoons thin soy sauce
1 tablespoon plus 1 teaspoon Asian sesame oil
1 egg white
1 tablespoon cornstarch
1/2 teaspoon freshly ground black pepper, plus additional to taste
4 dried Chinese black mushrooms
1/4 cup bamboo shoots
1/2 pound soba noodles
6 cups Basic Chicken Broth (page 22)
Salt to taste
2 scallions (green and white parts), minced, for garnish

In a food processor, combine the shrimp, flounder, pork, soy, 1 teaspoon of the sesame oil, egg white, cornstarch, and 1/2 teaspoon of the black pepper. Process to a fine paste. Wet your hands and form the paste into small meatballs. In a small bowl, soak the mushrooms in 1/3 cup of hot water. Drain, reserving the soaking liquid, then remove the stems and discard them. Slice the mushrooms into thin shreds. Slice the bamboo shoots into fine matchsticks.

Bring a large pot of water to a boil. Add the soba noodles and cook for 5 to 8 minutes, until just done. Drain and rinse with cold running water. Set aside.

In a stainless-steel or coated-aluminum wok, bring the chicken broth and mushroom soaking liquid to a simmer. Add the meatballs and cook for about 5 minutes, or until they feel firm when pressed with a fork. Add the noodles, mushrooms, and bamboo shoots. Stir to mix well, and cook until the noodles are warmed through. Season with salt and black pepper. Sprinkle with the scallions, drizzle with the remaining sesame oil, and serve.

Seafood Soup with Garland Chrysanthemum

Several varieties of edible chrysanthemum are grown, but the broad-leaf variety, also known as the chop suey vegetable, is the most popular in China and Japan because of its distinctive flavor. The leaves are usually harvested young to keep their sweet flavor. In this recipe, garland chrysanthemum perfumes the soup, making it a complement to the seafood. If you can't find garland chrysanthemum, another leafy green may be substituted; the soup will take on the flavor of the vegetable you use—and you will have come up with a new dish. You may substitute chicken or fish broth for the dashi. This recipe makes a generous quantity to serve a crowd; the wok allows you to stir the soup easily without breaking up the delicate pieces of fish.

SERVES 8

6 cups Dashi (page 24)
¼ cup soy sauce
¼ cup mirin
2 tablespoons sake
1 teaspoon Japanese pepper *(sansho)*
2 cups water
1½ pounds garland chrysanthemum
½ pound wheat noodles, cooked
16 littleneck clams, scrubbed
¼ pound medium shrimp, shelled and deveined
2 whole squid, cleaned and cut into 1-inch-wide pieces
¼ pound scallops, adductor muscles removed, if desired
¾ pound red snapper fillets, cut into 2-inch pieces

In a large stainless-steel or coated-aluminum wok, combine the dashi, soy, mirin, sake, *sansho*, and water. Bring to a boil, reduce the heat, and simmer for 5 to 10 minutes. Meanwhile, wash the garland chrysanthemum; trim off and discard the stems; and separate the leaves.

Add the chrysanthemum leaves and noodles to the broth, stirring to mix well. Return the soup to a simmer and add the clams and shrimp; simmer for 3 minutes, then add the squid, scallops, and snapper. Keep the seafood submerged just below the surface of the broth. Stir gently to distribute the seafood evenly. Cook for another 5 minutes, or until the fish fillets flake easily and the clams have just opened. Do not overcook. Serve the soup in deep bowls and provide a large bowl for diners to discard the shells.

Shrimp and Rice Stick Noodle Soup

This typical light soup makes a perfect quick lunch, and here again the wok offers decided advantages. Because the rice stick noodles are precooked, the generous surface of the wok helps them to heat through quickly without overcooking. Blending the noodles, shrimp, and broth is also a cinch.

SERVES 4

½ **pound rice stick noodles**
4 **cups Fish and Shrimp Broth (page 24)**
1 **quarter-sized slice minced peeled fresh ginger**
2 **dried hot peppers, crumbled**
1 **tablespoon coarsely chopped cilantro**
¾ **pound medium shrimp, peeled and deveined**
2 **scallions (white and green parts), cut into 2-inch pieces**
Salt and freshly ground black pepper to taste
Cilantro sprigs, for garnish

Soak the rice sticks in warm water for about 15 minutes, until soft; drain.

In a stainless-steel or coated-aluminum wok, combine the broth, ginger, hot peppers, and cilantro. Bring to a boil, reduce the heat to low, and simmer for 5 minutes. Add the shrimp and cook for 1 to 2 minutes over low heat, until the shrimp turn pink. Add the scallions and rice stick noodles, and cook for 30 seconds. Season with salt and pepper, and stir to mix well. Spoon into bowls and garnish each with cilantro sprigs.

Curried Mussel Bisque

This is my version of billy-bi, the famous French mussel bisque. Although it is delicious, I have always felt it was far too rich. Here I have blended Eastern and Western flavors and techniques for a lighter bisque. The amount of butter in the recipe is generous, but remember, only a minimal amount of cream is used. If fat is a big concern, the quantity of butter can be reduced by as much as half and the bisque will still be delicious. The mussels cook quickest and most uniformly in one or two layers, making a wok the perfect pan for this soup.

SERVES 6

3 pounds mussels
3 cups dry white wine
1 cup minced shallots
¼ cup minced parsley
1 tablespoon fresh thyme leaves, coarsely minced
8 tablespoons unsalted butter
1 cup water
2 teaspoons vegetable oil
1 tablespoon Madras curry powder
½ teaspoon turmeric
4 Kaffir lime leaves
2 tablespoons anisette
¼ cup heavy cream
2 teaspoons salt
1 teaspoon freshly ground black pepper

Using a stiff brush, scrub the mussels under cold running water. Discard any that have cracked or opened shells. In a stainless-steel or coated-aluminum wok, combine the wine, shallots, parsley, thyme, butter, and water. Cover and bring to a boil. Reduce the heat and simmer for about 10 minutes, or until the broth is aromatic. Add the mussels, cover, and cook over medium-high heat. After 5 minutes, uncover the wok and, with a pair of tongs, begin removing the mussels to a plate as they open; do not overcook the mussels. Discard any that do not open. When the mussels are cool enough to handle, remove from the shells and discard the shells. Strain the broth through cheesecloth. Discard the solids. Wipe out the wok with paper towels.

In the wok, heat the oil over medium heat and stir-fry the curry powder and turmeric for about 30 seconds, until aromatic. Add the mussel broth and lime leaves, then bring to a simmer and cook for 10 minutes. Remove the lime leaves and discard them. Add the anisette, cream, salt, and pepper. Simmer another minute, then add the mussels and cook just until the mussels are heated through. Serve hot.

Rosy Amaranth and Fish Soup

Amaranth added to a vegetable broth contributes a faint sweetness and rosy color. In this recipe, I've used monkfish for its lobsterlike texture, but any kind of white fish will work fine. Because the fish is best cooked in a single layer, a wide wok is the perfect pot to use.

SERVES 6

1 pound red amaranth
6 cups Dashi (page 24) or Basic Vegetable Broth (page 17)
2 slices fresh ginger (each about the size of a quarter)
1 whole scallion, trimmed
1 tablespoon sake
1 tablespoon thin soy sauce
1 pound monkfish, cut into bite-size pieces
1 teaspoon Japanese pepper *(sansho)*
Salt to taste

Wash the amaranth; remove the stems and discard them.

In a stainless-steel or coated-aluminum wok, combine the broth, ginger, and scallion. Bring to a boil, reduce the heat, and simmer for 15 minutes. Discard the ginger and scallion. Add the sake, soy, and monkfish in a single layer. Cook for 5 to 8 minutes, until the fish just begins to turn opaque. Add the amaranth and continue cooking for another 5 minutes, until the vegetable wilts and becomes tender and the broth turns pink. Add the pepper and salt, and serve.

Scallop Ravioli in Ginger Broth

The scallop mousse filling for these ravioli is light and low in fat because I use an Asian technique to bind the scallops—adding egg whites and cornstarch, with only a very little bit of cream. In fact, you could leave the cream out altogether. The ginger flavor in the broth is a nice counterpoint to the sweetness of the scallops. Use a wok to poach the ravioli so they have plenty of room to float as they rise to the surface. Do not let them boil rapidly or touch as they cook—they are fragile and will break apart.

SERVES 6

For the Filling

1/2 **pound sea scallops**
3 **slices peeled fresh ginger (each about the size of a quarter)**
1 **egg white**
1 **tablespoon cornstarch**
1 **teaspoon salt**
1/4 **teaspoon cayenne, or to taste**
1 **tablespoon dry white wine**
2 **tablespoons heavy cream**

24 **thin wonton skins**
1 **egg beaten with 1 tablespoon water**
8 **to 10 cups water**
3 **cups Ginger Broth (page 20)**
1/4 **cup finely julienned scallions (green part only)**
1 **tablespoon finely julienned peeled fresh ginger**

Prepare the filling: In a food processor, mince the scallops and ginger to a smooth puree. Add the egg white, cornstarch, salt, cayenne, white wine, and cream, and pulse until smooth.

On a work surface, lay out the wonton skins. Spoon about 2 teaspoons of the filling onto the center of each wonton skin. Brush the edges with a little egg mixture and fold over to form triangles. Set on a clean towel, then cover with another towel until ready to use.

Bring the water to a simmer in a stainless-steel or coated-aluminum wok. Gently poach the ravioli for about 5 minutes, until the filling sets. The ravioli will rise to the top when they are done. While the ravioli cook, heat the ginger broth in a separate saucepan. Ladle the broth into serving bowls and slip 4 ravioli per serving into each bowl. Scatter the julienned scallions and ginger over the soup, and serve immediately.

3

braising
and stewing

In the days of hearth cooking, braising was the most typical cooking technique in many cultures. Today it has become less common, which is a pity, since few techniques produce food more savory, tender, and deeply flavored. ● Whereas in boiling or poaching, meat is submerged in liquid (usually only slightly flavored) and cooked relatively quickly, in braising (and stewing), the food stands only partially in flavored liquid and gently simmers, allowing for a full exchange of flavors. Braising is the best technique to use with less tender cuts. The long, slow cooking process breaks down the tissue and tenderizes the meat, while allowing flavors from the cooking liquid to be fully absorbed. ● Another advantage of braising that I particularly appreciate is that once a braised dish is started, it can be left to simmer on its own, with only an occasional peep at the pot to make sure the liquid has not all cooked away. Braised dishes keep very well, and many, in fact, improve when left overnight. They can be refrigerated for several days and will freeze well for up to several months. Coming home to a braised entrée stored in your freezer and ready to heat is a welcome that most of us would appreciate.

The most efficient pan for preparing a braise or stew is one that is wide and has low sides. For cooks familiar with the French kitchen, the obvious choice would be the shallow, low-sided pan known as a *rondeau*. But these pans, usually of heavy steel or copper, are extremely expensive. Fortunately, the wok has all the features I want in a *rondeau,* at a much gentler price. The wok should be covered during braising, with its own lid or one improvised by cutting paper or parchment to fit inside the pan. During the braising process, it is desirable for the liquid to cook down so the flavors will intensify, and the wider surface of the wok allows you to achieve this without having to reduce rapidly at the end. The level of the cooking liquid should, however, be checked occasionally during braising, as the food should always be at least partially submerged.

With its wide opening and sloping sides, the wok not only easily accommodates bulky ingredients, which are hard to stir and mix in a deep pot like a Dutch oven, but conducts heat with optimum efficiency, so that the food cooks evenly. Stirring and mixing the bulky ingredients for Hot and Sour Seafood Stew (page 72), for example, can be a pain when everything is squashed into a tall narrow saucepan; some seafood will always end up a touch overcooked. The same is true of chicken and duck dishes. Trying to find a pan of suitable shape and size to prepare Braised Fish with Turmeric and White Wine (page 70) will put off anyone who does not possess a complete *batterie,* but reach for your trusty wok and your fish will be cooked in the time it takes for you to find that special pan. If you are making a curry mixture from scratch, the dry-roasting of the spices should also be done in a wok, where the bigger surface allows the spices to roast quickly and evenly.

Many recipes in this chapter call for an initial stir-frying of the seasoning vegetables. When I use a wok for this, I can go from stir-frying to braising without changing pans. The different spices that produce the complex flavors in curries, red-braised dishes, and other Asian stews can easily be stirred and blended in the wok. Again, thanks to the shape of the pan, the meat, poultry, or fish cooks in shallow layers, which allows the flavors to meld and become more evenly distributed.

We do not usually associate braising with wok cooking. My friends and professional colleagues are often taken aback when presented with braised dishes that I prepared in a wok. The technique is uncommon enough that the dishes are not often recognized as Asian. Try wok-braising and you, too, will be delighted by the results.

vegetables

Braised Vegetables

The natural sweetness of the vegetables and the delicate flavor of miso make a perfect match in this vegetarian dish. If you cannot find green daikon, use the more common white variety or regular turnips. I like the crunch that soy sprouts add to the dish. Do not substitute regular bean sprouts, as they tend to over-cook easily. Serve this as a side dish or as an entrée over rice.

SERVES 6 TO 8

1 green daikon (about 1½ pounds)
1 small jicama (about 1 pound)
2 carrots
2 cups bamboo shoots, cut into 2-inch pieces
1 cup raw peanuts
3 tablespoons white miso
1 teaspoon minced peeled fresh ginger
2 cups water
1 pound soybean sprouts
Salt and freshly ground black pepper to taste
2 teaspoons Asian sesame oil

Peel the daikon and cut it into 1-inch-thick slices. Peel the jicama and cut it into 1-inch cubes. Peel the carrots and cut them into 1-inch-thick chunks.

In a stainless-steel or coated-aluminum wok, combine the daikon, jicama, carrots, bamboo shoots, peanuts, miso, ginger, and water. Bring to a simmer and cook for 10 minutes. Add the soybean sprouts and continue cooking for another 10 minutes, until the vegetables are tender but still crisp. Season with salt and pepper. Drizzle with the sesame oil and serve.

Braised Baby Bok Choy

For this dish, you can use either the regular variety of bok choy, with white stalks and dark green leaves, or the type known as Shanghai bok choy, with jade green leaves and stalks—buy the variety that is freshest at the market. Small individual lettuces also work well here. Bok choy tends to be gritty between the stalks, so wash the vegetables in a sinkful of tepid water; the grit sinks to the bottom with only one or two changes of water. You can also add a few drops of oil to the water as an additional aid to removing the sand.

SERVES 8 AS A SIDE DISH

8 small heads of baby bok choy
1 teaspoon vegetable oil
1 teaspoon minced peeled fresh ginger
1 scallion (white part only), minced
½ teaspoon ground cumin
2 cups Basic Chicken Broth (page 22)
Salt and freshly ground black pepper to taste
2 teaspoons cornstarch mixed with 1 tablespoon cold water

Wash the bok choy well in lots of tepid water, making sure that all the sand and grit are removed. Drain in a colander.

In a carbon-steel wok, heat the oil over high heat until just smoking. Add the ginger and scallion, and stir-fry for 30 seconds. Add the cumin and stir; then add the bok choy in a single layer. Add the broth, salt, and pepper, and bring to a simmer. Braise the vegetables for 20 to 30 minutes, or until tender. With a slotted spoon, remove the bok choy to a serving platter. Add the cornstarch mixture to the stock, bring to a boil, and cook for about 1 minute, until the sauce thickens. Adjust the seasoning, pour the sauce over the vegetables, and serve.

Braised Lettuce and Sugar Snaps

This is my variation of a classic French way with lettuce. I usually prepare it with the first tender young peas of the season, but because this season is so brief, I have substituted sugar snaps, which are around a little longer. The Chinese "mirepoix" of ginger and scallions gives this dish an Asian touch.

SERVES 2

1 head of lettuce, preferably romaine
2 tablespoons unsalted butter
2 scallions (green and white parts), minced
1/2 teaspoon minced peeled fresh ginger
4 ounces sugar snap peas, strings removed
2 tablespoons heavy cream
1/2 teaspoon salt
1/4 teaspoon freshly ground black pepper
Pinch of sugar

Wash the lettuce and cut the leaves into narrow ribbons.

In a small stainless-steel or coated-aluminum wok set over low heat, melt the butter, add the scallions and ginger, and stir; then add the peas, cream, salt, pepper, and sugar. Scatter the shredded lettuce over the peas. Cover the wok and cook for 5 to 10 minutes, until the peas are tender and the lettuce is meltingly sweet.

Eggplant in Oyster Sauce

This simple eggplant dish is easy to make and rewarms well. At the end of summer, when this vegetable is plentiful, make a double batch. I prefer to use Asian eggplants because they are less seedy. If you can't get these, my next choice would be the small Italian eggplants. Don't overcook the Asian eggplants—properly done, they will hold their shape well and not become mushy.

SERVES 4

1 pound Asian eggplant
1 tablespoon vegetable oil
2 teaspoons minced peeled fresh ginger
2 garlic cloves, minced
1 scallion (green and white parts), minced
2 tablespoons oyster sauce
1 tablespoon dark soy sauce
¾ cup water
1 teaspoon freshly ground black pepper

Cut the eggplant into 2-inch-thick pieces.

In a carbon-steel wok, heat the oil over high heat until just smoking. Add the ginger, garlic, and scallion, and cook for 10 seconds. Add the eggplant, oyster sauce, dark soy, water, and pepper. Bring the liquid to a simmer and braise the eggplant for 20 minutes, or until tender.

Taro Braised with Red Miso

These hairy, oval-shaped little tubers are a favorite in Chinatown in fall, when they are plentiful. As children, we used to have them peeled, boiled, and dipped in sugar for an after-school snack. This dish makes a nice change from potatoes, and is tasty enough to serve as a vegetarian main course.

SERVES 4

1 pound small taro roots (about 4), or 1 large root
2 tablespoons vegetable oil
1 garlic clove, minced
1 tablespoon red miso
1 tablespoon thin soy sauce
2 tablespoons plum wine
2 umeboshi plums, mashed
2 teaspoons sugar
1½ cups water

Peel the taro. Cut in half if small, cut into 2-inch chunks if large.

In a stainless-steel or coated-aluminum wok, heat the oil over medium heat until just smoking. Add the garlic and cook for a few seconds. Add the miso, soy, plum wine, umeboshi plums, sugar, and water. Bring to a boil and add the taro. Reduce the heat and simmer for 30 to 45 minutes, until the taro is cooked through. Add a little water during the cooking, if necessary.

Malaysian Curried Potatoes and Green Beans

You don't have to use exotic produce to make an unusual dish. This vegetarian curry is quick, easy, and prepared with readily available ingredients. You can have dinner on the table in under an hour when you serve this with a little rice; make it one day ahead and the flavor will be even better.

SERVES 4

2 pounds Red Bliss potatoes
1 tablespoon vegetable oil
1 tablespoon minced shallots
1 yellow onion, coarsely minced
2 garlic cloves
1 tablespoon minced peeled fresh ginger
2 tablespoons Madras curry powder
1 cup coconut milk
2 cups Basic Vegetable Broth (page 17) or water
2 teaspoons salt
1 teaspoon freshly ground black pepper
1 pound fresh young green beans, trimmed

Wash the potatoes under cold running water. Peel and cut into 2-inch chunks.

In a carbon-steel wok, heat the oil over medium heat until just smoking. Add the shallots, onion, garlic, and ginger, and stir-fry for 5 minutes, or until the onion is wilted. Add the curry and cook for 30 seconds, until aromatic. Add the coconut milk, broth, potatoes, salt, and pepper. Bring to a simmer and cook over low heat for 15 to 20 minutes, until the potatoes are tender. Add the green beans and cook for another 10 minutes, or until the beans are just done.

eggs and tofu

Curried Eggs

Growing up in a family of six children, we often had unexpected guests for meals, as one or the other of us would invariably ask a friend to stay for lunch or dinner. Any dish featuring eggs as the main ingredient was popular with the cook—as this was an easy way to accommodate extra diners. Eggs are a great favorite of mine, so I often asked for this dish. Carrots, peas, or turnips can also be added to stretch this curry even further.

SERVES 4

6 to 8 large eggs
1½ tablespoons vegetable oil
1 medium onion, finely chopped
2 garlic cloves, minced
2 teaspoons minced peeled fresh ginger
3 tablespoons Red Curry Paste (page 191)
1 teaspoon ground turmeric
¾ cup whole milk
Salt to taste

Place the eggs in a single layer in a saucepan. Cover with cold water, then bring to a boil and immediately turn off the heat. Cover tightly and let stand for 10 to 12 minutes. Remove the eggs from the hot water and refresh them in cold water. Peel the eggs and set them aside.

In a stainless-steel or coated-aluminum wok, heat the oil over medium heat until just smoking. Add the onion, garlic, and ginger, and stir-fry for about 5 minutes, until the onion is wilted. Add the curry paste and turmeric, and cook for 1 minute, stirring to prevent burning. Add the milk. Season with salt and cook over low heat for 15 to 20 minutes, or until the sauce thickens. *The sauce may be prepared up to this point and held.*

Cut the eggs in half lengthwise and add to the curry sauce. Cooking for another 3 to 5 minutes to heat the eggs through; spoon the sauce over the eggs to coat them well as they cook. Serve hot.

Tofu and Wild Mushrooms

Fresh wild mushrooms take this dish from ordinary to luxurious. The woodsy flavor of the mushrooms is enhanced by the *fu yue*, which is bean curd pickled in rice wine and salt. You can recognize it by its ivory color. Sold in jars, *fu yue* comes plain or flavored with hot chilies; the spicy version will have flecks of chili in it. *Fu yue* can be eaten straight out of the jar as a side dish or used as an ingredient. During the war years, as refugees in Macao, we could not get any butter, so we often spread *fu yue* on toast—something for which we acquired a fondness. Even today I sometimes eat *fu yue* on toast for a quick breakfast—and save on the butter calories. For a treat, add a dozen oysters to this dish. Serve this with white rice.

SERVES 4 TO 6

1 pound firm tofu
8 dried black mushrooms
1 large portobello mushroom
4 ounces each fresh shiitake, cremini, and oyster mushrooms
1 tablespoon vegetable oil
1 tablespoon minced peeled fresh ginger
1 tablespoon minced scallion (green and white parts)
2 garlic cloves, minced
3 tablespoons dark soy sauce
¼ cup Madeira
2 squares *fu yue* (pickled bean curd)
Salt and freshly ground black pepper to taste

Cut the tofu into 2-inch squares. In a small bowl, soak the black mushrooms in 2 cups of warm water for about 15 minutes, or until soft. Clean the fresh mushrooms with damp paper towels. Remove and discard the stems of the portobello and shiitake mushrooms. Cut the portobello into pieces about 1 inch square. Halve the shiitake and cremini mushrooms, and separate the oyster mushrooms into smaller sections. Drain the black mushrooms, reserving the soaking liquid. Remove the stems and discard them. If the black mushrooms are very big, cut them in half.

In a carbon-steel wok, heat the oil over high heat until just smoking. Add the ginger, scallion, and garlic, and stir-fry for 30 seconds, or until aromatic. Add the soy sauce, Madeira, and *fu yue,* mashing the *fu yue* to break it up. Add the tofu, mushrooms, and soaking liquid. Bring to a simmer, reduce the heat to low, and braise for 30 to 40 minutes, or until the tofu has absorbed flavor. If the dish becomes too dry, add a little water. Season to taste with salt and pepper, and serve.

Braised Tofu Sticks, Vegetables, and *Nam Yue*

When I was growing up in Hong Kong, there was a famous Buddhist monastery in Shatin, at that time a little village in the New Territories. Shatin in the '50s and '60s was typical of the little farming villages that today you will find only in China. The monastery ran a famous vegetarian restaurant, and I can remember sitting in the garden in the summer and eating the most sumptuous vegetarian banquets. Traditional Buddhist cuisine offers many versions of this vegetarian tofu dish, which uses both dried and fresh vegetables. My updated version calls for only fresh root vegetables that are easily available, and retains the special flavor that *nam yue* (red preserved bean curd) provides. Long, slow braising gives the flavors of the vegetables and sauce a chance to meld. In the fall, be sure to use fresh pumpkin instead of the papaya or winter squash. *Nam yue* is sold in jars and keeps indefinitely in the refrigerator. Serve this dish over white rice.

SERVES 8 TO 10

4 ounces dried tofu sticks
1 pound young carrots
2 pounds green papaya, winter squash *(nam kwa)*, **or pumpkin**
1 tablespoon vegetable oil
1 tablespoon minced peeled fresh ginger
¼ cup dry sherry
2 tablespoons dark soy sauce
2 tablespoons *nam yue* **(red preserved bean curd)**
2 teaspoons sugar
½ cup raw peanuts
4 cups shredded Chinese cabbage
2 to 4 cups Basic Vegetable Broth (page 17)
Salt to taste

In a bowl of hot water, soak the tofu sticks until soft. Drain and cut into 3-inch-long pieces. Peel the carrots and cut on the diagonal into 1-inch pieces. Peel the papaya and cut into 2-inch chunks; you should have about 4 cups.

Heat the oil in a stainless-steel or coated-aluminum wok. Add the ginger and sauté for 30 seconds, until aromatic. Add the sherry, soy sauce, *nam yue,* and sugar. Mash the *nam yue* to break it up, and mix to blend well. Add the softened tofu sticks and the prepared vegetables. Stir to mix. Add the peanuts, shredded cabbage, and enough broth to cover. Bring to a simmer and cook for about 45 minutes, or until all the vegetables are tender. Season to taste with salt.

Red-Braised "Duck"

Unlike Western vegetarians, Buddhist chefs aim to make their vegetarian entrées taste like meat, often imitating familiar meat dishes with meat substitutes such as *seitan* or bean curd. For example, when braising tofu to simulate duck, chefs will add exactly the same spices and flavorings as those in the duck version. In this recipe I have used frozen tofu because the spongy texture absorbs the rich flavor of the sauce and provides a "meatiness" to this vegetarian entrée that duplicates a traditional red-braised duck dish. For a hearty meal, serve over white rice.

SERVES 4

1 pound firm tofu, frozen for at least 24 hours and thawed
1 green daikon (2 to 3 pounds)
2 teaspoons vegetable oil
1 tablespoon minced shallots
1 teaspoon minced peeled fresh ginger
2 tablespoons dark soy sauce
¼ teaspoon five-spice powder
1 teaspoon Szechwan peppercorns
1 teaspoon salt
1 teaspoon freshly ground black pepper
2 cups Basic Vegetable Broth (page 17)

Cut the tofu into 2-inch cubes and squeeze out any excess water. Peel the daikon and cut into 2-inch cubes.

In a carbon-steel wok, heat the oil over medium heat until just smoking. Add the shallots and ginger, and sauté for 1 minute, until wilted and aromatic. Add the tofu and daikon, stir to mix, then add the soy, five-spice powder, Szechwan peppercorns, salt, pepper, and broth. Bring to a boil, reduce the heat, and simmer for 30 to 40 minutes, or until the daikon is tender and the tofu is full of flavor. Serve hot.

Pressed Tofu Chili

Gently pressing tofu to eliminate some of the water gives it a firmer, meatier texture and makes the tofu heartier. The strong flavors of chili go well with tofu to produce a healthy meatless entrée that is also very quick to make. By crumbling the pressed tofu, I get a texture that very closely resembles that of ground meat. If you like beans, go ahead and add some. Be sure to use a good chili powder. My favorite is one made with Hatch chilies from New Mexico.

SERVES 4 TO 6

2 pounds firm tofu
2 tablespoons vegetable oil
1 medium onion, chopped
4 garlic cloves, minced
3 tablespoons chili powder
1 teaspoon ground cumin
½ teaspoon dried oregano
1 tablespoon tomato paste
3 cups water
1 teaspoon freshly ground black pepper
1 tablespoon Tabasco sauce (optional)
1 tablespoon cornmeal mixed with ¼ cup cold water
Salt to taste
1 tablespoon cilantro, coarsely chopped

Place the tofu on a board positioned with one end slightly elevated. Cover the tofu with another board or plate, and place a weight, such as a heavy can, on top. Let the tofu drain for at least 1 hour. (Pressed tofu can be stored in the refrigerator for up to 1 week.)

Place the pressed tofu in a large shallow bowl. With a potato masher, crumble the tofu until it has the consistency of ground meat.

In a carbon-steel wok, heat the oil and stir-fry the onion and garlic for 1 minute, until just wilted. Add the chili powder, cumin, oregano, tomato paste, and water, and mix well. Add the tofu, black pepper, and Tabasco sauce, if desired. Bring to a boil, reduce the heat, and simmer for 20 minutes.

Add the cornmeal mixture, bring the chili to a boil, and cook until it thickens. Season with salt to taste. Stir in the cilantro, and serve.

White-Braised Chicken and Cucumber

As combined in this dish, cucumbers and Chinese celery provide not only flavor but a built-in garnish. Substitute a handful of watercress or spinach leaves if you can't get Chinese celery. The white sauce is made the Asian way, with miso and stock in place of milk or cream.

SERVES 4

1 medium onion
4 whole cloves
2 cups Basic Chicken Broth (page 22)
1 slice fresh ginger (about the size of a quarter)
2 whole, bone-in chicken breasts
1 tablespoon white miso
1 teaspoon freshly ground white pepper
2 cucumbers
4 Chinese celery stalks, with leaves
1 tablespoon kosher salt plus additional for final seasoning
1 tablespoon cornstarch mixed with $\frac{1}{4}$ cup cold water

Peel the onion and stick it with the cloves. Pour the broth into a stainless-steel or coated-aluminum wok, add the onion and ginger, and bring the liquid to a boil. Add the chicken, miso, and white pepper, and simmer for 20 minutes, until the chicken is tender and cooked through.

Meanwhile, peel the cucumbers, cut them in half lengthwise, and remove the seeds with a teaspoon. Cut the cucumbers into half-moon shapes about $\frac{1}{2}$ inch thick. Separate the celery stalks from the leaves and cut the stalks into $\frac{1}{2}$-inch pieces. Coarsely chop the leaves. Fill a bowl with ice and water. Bring a large saucepan of water to a boil, add the tablespoon of kosher salt, and blanch the cucumber pieces for about 10 seconds, just until they turn jade green. Remove them immediately with a strainer and plunge them into ice water to cool completely. Repeat with the celery stalks. Drain the cooled vegetables.

With a slotted spoon, remove the chicken breasts from the broth. Let them cool and remove the skin and bones. Cut each breast in half so you have 4 pieces. Return the chicken to the broth, add the cucumber and celery stalks, and cook for 5 minutes, until heated through. Add the cornstarch mixture, stir to blend, and simmer for 1 minute, until the sauce thickens. Season with salt to taste, sprinkle the celery leaves on top, and serve.

Thai-Style Green Duck Curry

Ordinarily, a Thai duck curry would be made of pieces of duck with the skin and bones attached. I use duck breasts with the skin, bones, and all visible fat removed, which lowers the fat content considerably while keeping all the delicious flavor. You can add more jalapeños if you want your curry really spicy. If you can't get Thai basil, leave it out. (Italian basil makes a poor substitute; it just does not have the same flavor.) Serve this dish with white rice.

SERVES 4

2 whole boneless duck breasts (each about 2 pounds)
1 tablespoon vegetable oil
1 medium onion, chopped
2 garlic cloves, minced
1 tablespoon minced peeled fresh ginger
2 scallions (green and white parts), minced
3 jalapeños, seeded and minced
¼ cup cilantro leaves, minced
½ teaspoon ground coriander
½ teaspoon ground cumin
½ teaspoon ground cardamom
½ cup coconut milk (see Note)
1 cup nonfat yogurt
1 cup Basic Chicken Broth (page 22)
1 tablespoon fish sauce (*nuoc mam* or *nam pla*)
½ cup Thai basil leaves, slivered
Salt to taste

Remove the skin from the duck breasts and trim any visible fat. Cut the breats into strips about ½ inch wide and set them aside.

In a stainless-steel or coated-aluminum wok, heat the oil over medium heat until just smoking. Add the onion, garlic, ginger, and scallions, and stir-fry for 1 minute, until wilted. Add the jalapeños, cilantro leaves, coriander, cumin, and cardamom. Sauté for about 10 seconds, or until the spices are aromatic. Add the coconut milk, yogurt, broth, and fish sauce. Stir to blend. Bring to a simmer and braise over low heat for 30 minutes, until the sauce is smooth and creamy; do not boil, or the sauce will curdle.

Add the duck and the basil leaves. Cook for another 15 minutes, or until the duck is tender. Season with salt to taste, and serve.

Note: Look for A Taste of Thai Lite Coconut Milk, which has 70 percent less fat than regular coconut milk.

Braised Duck and Sweet Potatoes with *Nam Yue*

As a walk through Chinatown will illustrate, duck is very popular with Chinese cooks, who prepare it in many different ways. When it is braised, the fat is rendered into the sauce and helps to keep the meat tender and moist. In this hearty dish, *nam yue,* or red fermented bean curd, gives the duck a particular richness. *Nam yue* is pickled in red rice wine lees, rice wine, and salt, and has a crumbly texture similar to that of ripe Camembert. There is no mistaking its special flavor. This dish freezes well. Make it ahead of time and thoroughly degrease it when cool.

SERVES 4

1 duck (about 5 pounds)
1 pound sweet potatoes
1 tablespoon minced peeled fresh ginger
2 garlic cloves, minced
¼ cup dry sherry
2 tablespoons *nam yue*, mashed
½ teaspoon five-spice powder
½ cup dark soy sauce
2 tablespoons thin soy sauce
1 teaspoon freshly ground black pepper
1 tablespoon (lightly packed) brown sugar
1½ cups water
4 scallions (green and white parts), cut into 2-inch pieces
2 tablespoons cornstarch mixed with ¼ cup cold water

Trim all excess fat from the duck, and cut the duck in half. Remove the backbone and set it aside. Cut the duck into 6 pieces: 2 breast halves, 2 thighs, and 2 legs. Peel the sweet potatoes and cut them into 3-inch chunks.

Heat a carbon-steel wok over medium heat. Add a few pieces of the duck, skin-side down, and brown, turning once. Remove the pieces when they are nicely colored, and brown the remaining pieces. Drain off the fat, reserving 1 tablespoon. Add the ginger and garlic, and sauté for 30 seconds over medium heat. Add the sherry, *nam yue*, five-spice powder, dark and thin soy sauces, pepper, sugar, and water. Add the duck pieces and the reserved backbone, and bring the liquid to a simmer. Cover the wok and braise the duck for 20 to 25 minutes. Add the sweet potato and cook for another 30 minutes, until the duck and sweet potatoes are tender. With a slotted spoon, remove the duck and potatoes to a serving dish. Degrease the sauce. Add the scallions and return the sauce to a boil; add the cornstarch mixture and cook for about 1 minute, or until the sauce thickens. Pour it over the duck and serve.

meat

Red-Braised Pork with Fresh Pineapple

"Wonderful!" was the comment scribbled in the margin of this recipe when my friend and colleague, Donna Adams, tested it. The dish improves if prepared ahead of time and reheated. The pork freezes very well, but the pineapple does not, so add the fruit just before serving. You must use fresh pineapple, as the acidity of the fresh fruit provides the balance needed in the sauce. Serve this dish with white rice.

SERVES 6

1 tablespoon vegetable oil
3 pounds pork butt, cut into 1½-inch cubes
1 tablespoon minced peeled fresh ginger
2 scallions (green and white parts), minced
1-inch piece of dried tangerine peel
½ teaspoon five-spice powder
½ cup dry sherry
3 tablespoons dark soy sauce
1 tablespoon sugar
1 cup water
1 small pineapple, peeled and cut into 1½-inch chunks
1 tablespoon cornstarch mixed with 2 tablespoons cold water

In a carbon-steel, stainless-steel, or coated-aluminum wok, heat the oil over high heat until just smoking. Add the pork in three batches and brown on all sides. Remove the meat to a plate. Add the ginger and scallions, and stir-fry for 30 seconds. Return the pork to the pan. Reduce the heat to medium and add the tangerine peel, five-spice powder, sherry, soy sauce, sugar, and water.

Bring to a boil, reduce the heat to low, then cover and simmer for 30 minutes. *The dish may be prepared up to this point and frozen.* Add the pineapple chunks and continue cooking for another 15 to 20 minutes, until the meat is tender when pricked with a fork. Using a slotted spoon, remove the pork and pineapple to a serving platter. Add the cornstarch mixture to the sauce, bring to a boil, and cook for 1 minute, until the sauce thickens. Pour the sauce over the pork and serve.

Braised Pork Chops

This was one of my favorite dishes as a child. When topped with a puff pastry crust, pork chops braised with potatoes, soy sauce, and hard-boiled eggs became "sea pie," pronounced with a definite Cantonese intonation by our Chinese cook. It was named after the English sea captains who were common visitors in the early days of the British colony of Hong Kong. Of course, there is nothing English about this filling. I have written this recipe so the dish can stand alone, but you could make it into sea pie if you like.

SERVES 6

6 loin pork chops (each about 1 inch thick)
2 teaspoons salt
1 teaspoon freshly ground black pepper
6 large dried Chinese black mushrooms
1 tablespoon vegetable oil
1 large onion, sliced
6 small white potatoes, peeled and halved
¼ cup thin soy sauce
1 tablespoon cornstarch mixed with 2 tablespoons cold water
3 hard-boiled eggs

Trim the pork chops of any excess fat. Sprinkle with the salt and pepper. In a small bowl, soak the mushrooms in ½ cup warm water for 15 minutes, until soft. Drain them, reserving the soaking liquid. Remove the discard and stems. Cut the mushrooms in half or quarter them if they are very large.

In a carbon-steel wok, heat the oil over medium heat until just smoking. Add the chops and brown lightly on each side; remove them to a plate. Add the onion and cook until wilted. Return the chops to the wok, add the mushrooms, mushroom liquid, potatoes, soy sauce, and enough water to just cover the chops. Simmer for 20 minutes, until the chops are tender and the potatoes are cooked through. Remove the chops and potatoes to a serving platter, and keep warm. Add the cornstarch mixture to the sauce, bring to a boil, and cook for 1 minute, until the sauce thickens. Cut the eggs in half and arrange them on the top of the chops. Pour the sauce over everything and serve.

Braised Baby Back Ribs

This dish can be prepared and served in one of the sandy pots that are often used for Chinese braises. These inexpensive pots are currently much in vogue, and they do make a good conversation piece, as they are brought directly to the table. Old wives believe that the sandy pot imparts a special flavor, and I must confess that I am partial to rice cooked this way. The disadvantage of these pots is that they chip and break easily—sometimes even before one can get them home. So more often than not, I simply use my trusty wok and the results are just as tasty.

SERVES 4

2 racks baby back ribs (each about 1 pound)
2 teaspoons minced fresh garlic
1 tablespoon minced peeled fresh ginger
2 scallions (green and white parts), minced
½ cup hoisin sauce
¼ cup dark soy sauce
1 tablespoon Asian sesame oil
2 teaspoons chili paste
1 cup dry white wine
3 cups water
2 red plums, seeded and quartered

Cut each rack in half. Place the ribs, in layers, in a stainless-steel or coated-aluminum wok. In a small bowl, combine the garlic, ginger, scallions, hoisin, soy sauce, sesame oil, chili paste, white wine, and water, and stir to blend well. Pour over the ribs and turn to coat well. There should be enough liquid to almost cover the ribs. Add the plums. Bring the liquid to a simmer, cover the wok, and cook for 45 minutes to 1 hour, or until the ribs are tender. Transfer the ribs to a deep serving platter and pour the sauce over them.

Vietnamese Pork Cooked in Sugar

Don't be fooled by the name; this pork is not too sweet—it's simply delicious, and almost too easy to be so good. It takes only five minutes to put these simple ingredients into the wok, where they braise slowly on their own, becoming moist and tender. The pork is browned slowly to render some of its fat, so no additional oil is required. Serve this dish with rice.

SERVES 4 TO 6

3 pounds pork butt (with some fat left on)
3 scallions (green and white parts), finely minced
4 cups water
1 tablespoon sugar
½ teaspoon freshly ground black pepper
½ teaspoon salt
1 to 2 tablespoons fish sauce *(nuoc mam or nam pla)*

Cut the pork into 1-inch cubes. Heat a carbon-steel wok over medium-low heat and brown the pork, a few pieces at a time, turning often. Remove to a plate. Pour off any excess fat. Add the scallions and stir-fry for 30 seconds, tossing frequently. Return the pork to the wok, add the water, sugar, black pepper, and salt. Bring to a boil, reduce the heat, and simmer for 45 minutes, or until the pork is tender. Most of the sauce will be absorbed by the pork. Stir in the fish sauce and serve.

Thai-Style Red Lamb Curry

Lamb is an uncommon ingredient in Asia, except in regions that have large Muslim communities, but I thought it would make a nice change from the usual beef in this curry. When winter squash is not in season, use eggplant, potatoes, or carrots. A typical can of unsweetened coconut milk yields 2 cups and this recipe calls for 4; if you find that amount too rich, you can replace up to 2 cups of the coconut milk with water, skim milk, or broth. Serve this curry over fragrant jasmine rice.

SERVES 4

4 cups unsweetened coconut milk
5 tablespoons Red Curry Paste (page 191)
2 pounds boneless lamb, cut into 1½-inch cubes
2 tablespoons fish sauce *(nuoc mam* or *nam pla)*
1 tablespoon brown sugar
2 pounds winter squash, peeled, seeded, and cut into chunks
4 Kaffir lime leaves
1 cup fresh Thai basil leaves
Salt to taste

In a stainless-steel or coated-aluminum wok, bring 1 cup of the coconut milk to a simmer. Cook for about 15 minutes, until it thickens and the oil beads on the top. Stir in the curry paste and simmer for 1 to 2 minutes, until aromatic. Add the lamb and toss to coat well. Add the remaining 3 cups of the coconut milk, the fish sauce, and sugar. Bring to a boil, then reduce the heat and simmer for 1 hour. Add the squash and lime leaves, and continue cooking for 15 to 20 minutes, or until the squash and the meat are tender. Remove the lime leaves and discard. Stir in half of the basil leaves and cook for another minute. Season with salt to taste. Sprinkle the remaining basil leaves over the top of the curry and serve.

Asian-Flavored Veal Shanks

Osso buco is a favorite with my family, and I nearly always prepare it the Italian way. I decided, however, to give the veal shanks an Asian slant for this book. Here they are flavored with fermented black beans and ginger, then cooked in a tightly covered wok so that all the flavor is retained. If you would like to make this a spicy dish, add the dried red chilies, or even fresh ones thinly sliced. For a fusion dinner, serve the shanks with a risotto made with Ginger Broth (page 20) and matchstick zucchini sautéed with miso.

SERVES 4

4 pieces veal shanks (cut as for osso buco; each about 2 inches
    thick)
2 tablespoons all-purpose flour
1 teaspoon freshly ground black pepper
2 tablespoons fermented black beans
1 tablespoon minced fresh ginger
2 tablespoons thin soy sauce
2 cups Basic Chicken Broth (page 22)
2 scallions (green and white parts), minced
4 dried red chilies, crumbled (optional)
2 teaspoons Asian sesame oil

Tie the veal shanks securely so they will hold their shape. Toss together the flour and black pepper, and dredge the shanks in the flour. Rinse the black beans in cold water and lightly mash them with the handle of a knife or cleaver.

Place the shanks, in a single layer, in a stainless-steel or coated-aluminum wok. Sprinkle with the black beans and ginger. Add the soy, chicken broth, half of the scallions, and chilies, if using. Bring to a boil, reduce the heat, and simmer for 1 1/2 hours, or until the shanks are meltingly tender. Add a little water if the sauce appears too dry. Sprinkle with the remaining scallions and the sesame oil, and serve.

Braised Bali-Style Beef

The first time I made this meal for an all-Indonesian menu, I couldn't believe how easy it was to get a great-tasting dish simply by throwing everything into a wok and braising the meat until it was tender. Sweet syrupy Indonesian soy sauce, called *ketjap manis,* is the flavor characteristic in this dish. You can make your own version by simmering 2 cups dark soy with 2 star anise pods and 2 tablespoons white or dark brown sugar. The spiciness of the dish can be adjusted to suit your own taste—simply add more chilies or use fewer. Bali beef is just as good when made ahead and reheated right before serving. A bed of bright green wilted vegetables, such as bok choy leaves, amaranth, or spinach, gives this dish a beautiful yin-yang look.

SERVES 6

1 tablespoon vegetable oil
4 garlic cloves, minced
1 tablespoon minced peeled fresh ginger
8 fresh red chilies, seeded and minced
2 teaspoons shrimp paste
3 pounds boneless beef chuck, trimmed and cut into 2-inch cubes
¼ cup *ketjap manis*
1 star anise pod
Juice of 1 lemon
Salt to taste

In a carbon-steel wok, heat the oil over high heat until just smoking. Add the garlic, ginger, chilies, and shrimp paste. Cook for 30 seconds, or until aromatic, stirring constantly to prevent burning. Add the beef and toss to coat well, then add the *ketjap manis,* star anise, and enough water to just cover the meat. Simmer for 1½ to 2 hours, until the meat is tender. Add more water during cooking if the dish appears too dry; at the end there should be only enough sauce to coat the meat. Stir in the lemon juice, season with salt to taste, and serve.

seafood

Braised Shrimp, Pork, and Jicama Meatballs with Tree Ears

Who doesn't love meatballs? This version is low in calories, as I have replaced some of the pork with shrimp and do not use an egg as a binder. This dish is best served with wheat noodles to sop up the soupy sauce, so you don't lose even a tiny bit of flavor.

SERVES 4

For the Meatballs
2 tablespoons dried tree ears *(wan yee)*
½ pound medium shrimp, peeled and deveined
½ pound lean ground pork
½ cup jicama, cut into ¼-inch cubes
1 teaspoon salt
1 tablespoon dark soy sauce
1 tablespoon Asian sesame oil
1 teaspoon sugar
1 teaspoon freshly ground black pepper
2 teaspoons cornstarch

For the Sauce
1 teaspoon vegetable oil
2 scallions (green and white parts), minced
1 cup chopped cilantro leaves
2 cups Basic Chicken Broth (page 22)
1½ tablespoons fish sauce *(nuoc mam* or *nam pla)*
Juice of 1 lime

Cilantro sprigs, for garnish (optional)

Prepare the meatballs: In a bowl, soak the tree ears in warm water for 10 to 15 minutes. Drain, rinse in cold water to remove any grit, drain again, and chop coarsely. Finely chop the shrimp, either by hand or in a food processor. In a large bowl, mix together the tree ears, shrimp, ground pork, jicama, soy, sesame oil, sugar, pepper, and cornstarch. Toss to mix well. Form the mixture into 12 meatballs about the size of golf balls and set aside.

Prepare the sauce: In a stainless-steel or coated-aluminum wok, heat the vegetable oil over medium heat. Add half of the scallions and toss for 10 seconds. Add half of the cilantro leaves, the chicken broth, fish sauce, and lime juice, and bring to a simmer.

Add the meatballs to the sauce and cook over low heat for 20 minutes, or until the meatballs are cooked through. Add the remaining scallions and cilantro leaves, and stir. Garnish with additional cilantro sprigs, if desired.

Ceylon-Style Curried Fish Steaks

Years ago, when I lived in London, I used to go to a little curry shop on Kensington High Street with a friend who grew up on a tea plantation in Ceylon. Highly spiced fish curry was the dish we ordered regularly, and I can still remember the taste of it. It was so hot, tears would run down our faces after a bite or two. To duplicate this very hot curry, add the optional chilies—and have plenty of ice-cold beer on hand to wash it down. Steamed basmati rice makes a good base for this dish.

SERVES 4

2 tablespoons vegetable oil
½ cup finely chopped onion
4 shallots, finely chopped
2 garlic cloves, minced
1 tablespoon minced peeled fresh ginger
3 tablespoons Sri Lankan Curry Paste (page 189)
1 teaspoon ground turmeric
1 2-inch-square tamarind pulp, soaked in ½ cup warm water
4 dried chilies, crumbled (optional)
4 cod or salmon steaks (each about ½ pound and 1½ inches thick)

In a carbon-steel wok, heat the oil over high heat until smoking. Add the onion, shallots, garlic, and ginger, and stir-fry until the onion is wilted. Add the curry paste and turmeric, and continue to fry, stirring to prevent burning. Add the tamarind pulp, its soaking liquid, and the chilies, if using. Reduce the heat to low and simmer for about 10 minutes. Add a little more water if the curry becomes dry. Add the fish steaks, cover, and cook for 10 minutes, or until the fish just begins to flake.

Braised Fish with Turmeric and White Wine

The flavors of this dish typify the fusion cooking of Macao, where my family comes from. Many of the ingredients are familiar, but the white wine clearly reflects Macao's Portuguese heritage. The strips of tomato, which make a nice garnish, are troublesome to prepare, so feel free to leave them out if you like.

SERVES 6

1 whole fish, such as snapper, sea bass, or Spanish mackerel (about 3 pounds)
1 tablespoon vegetable oil
6 whole scallions
2 teaspoons minced peeled fresh ginger
3 garlic cloves, minced
1 tablespoon ground turmeric
1 cup dry white wine
2 cups Fish and Shrimp Broth (page 24) or Basic Chicken Broth (page 22)
2 teaspoons salt
1 teaspoon freshly ground black pepper
4 plum tomatoes, for garnish

Rinse the fish and pat dry with paper towels. Make three shallow slashes about 3 inches long across one side of the fish; do not cut all the way through. Rub it all over, inside and out, with the oil and place on a plate. Fill a bowl with ice water, and bring a saucepan of water to a boil. Dip the scallions into the boiling water and immediately dip into the ice water to refresh them. Roll up each scallion into a wad about 2 inches long and tie, or cut the scallions into 2-inch pieces. Rub the fish all over with the ginger, garlic, and turmeric. Stuff the scallion bundles into the cavity of the fish and into each slash. Pour the white wine over the fish, cover with plastic wrap, and marinate in the refrigerator for 4 to 6 hours. (The fish may be kept in its marinade overnight.)

In a stainless-steel or coated-aluminum wok, heat the broth over low heat. Add the fish, salt, pepper, and any liquid on the plate. Bring to a simmer, cover the wok, and braise the fish for 20 to 30 minutes, or until it feels firm when gently pressed. Remove the fish to a platter and keep warm. Bring the sauce to a boil and cook for 10 minutes, until slightly reduced. Pour the sauce over the fish.

While the fish is cooking, blanch the tomatoes in boiling water. Refresh in ice water and peel. Quarter the tomatoes and discard the seeds. Cut the tomato pulp into thin strips and sprinkle over the fish.

Spicy Wine-Braised Jumbo Shrimp

Because shrimp cooks so quickly, you must use jumbo shrimp for this recipe; otherwise, the shrimp will overcook before they can absorb the taste of the sauce. The flavors are fiery and strong, but the sweetness of the shrimp is a nice contrast. The sauce cooks down quickly in the wok, gaining a syrupy consistency and coating the shrimp. Serve this dish with steamed white rice.

SERVES 4

1 tablespoon fermented black beans
2 teaspoons vegetable oil
3 tablespoons sliced shallots
4 garlic cloves, sliced
1 teaspoon slivered peeled fresh ginger
6 fresh red or green chilies, seeded and thinly sliced
1 tablespoon white miso
¾ cup sake
½ teaspoon Japanese pepper *(sansho)*
Pinch of sugar
½ cup water
1 pound jumbo shrimp, peeled and deveined

Rinse the black beans in warm water and drain. Mash them coarsely in a small bowl.

In a stainless-steel or coated-aluminum wok, heat the oil over medium heat until just smoking. Add the shallots, garlic, and ginger, and stir-fry for 1 minute. Add the black beans, chilies, miso, sake, Japanese pepper, sugar, and water. Bring to a boil, then reduce the heat and simmer for 5 minutes. Add the shrimp to the sauce and gently braise over low heat for 7 to 10 minutes, just until the shrimp turn pink and are cooked through.

Hot and Sour Seafood Stew

This hearty stew makes a great one-dish supper. Serve it with crusty peasant bread and a light green salad, or spoon it over mounds of white rice as the Asians do. You can make it less spicy and serve a dish of fiery sambal oelek on the side. Chicken broth combined with clam juice works fine in this recipe, but if you want a stronger seafood flavor, use Fish and Shrimp Broth (page 24).

SERVES 8

1 pound medium shrimp
2 pounds mussels
1 pound red snapper fillets, with skin left on
½ pound sea scallops
½ pound cleaned squid
2 limes
1 tablespoon vegetable oil
10 cups Fish and Shrimp Broth (page 24)
4 stalks lemongrass (white part only), cut into 1-inch lengths
6 Kaffir lime leaves
2 tablespoons fish sauce *(nuoc mam or nam pla)*
4 hot green chilies, slivered
2 fresh hot red chilies, slivered
¼ cup cilantro leaves, coarsely chopped
4 scallions (green and white parts), minced

Shell and devein the shrimp, reserving the shells. Scrub the mussels under cold running water and pull off the fibrous beards. Discard any that are open or cracked. Remove any pin bones from the fish and cut the fillets into 2-inch pieces. Remove the tough adductor muscles from the side of each scallop, if desired. Cut the squid into 1½-inch pieces. Peel the zest from 1 lime and juice both limes.

In a stainless-steel or coated-aluminum wok, heat the oil and stir-fry the shrimp shells over medium heat until they turn pink. Add the broth, lemongrass, lime leaves, fish sauce, green chilies, and lime zest. Bring to a simmer over medium heat, cover, and cook for about 20 minutes, or until the broth is flavorful. Strain the broth, return it to the wok, and discard the solids. Bring the broth back to a simmer over medium heat. Add the mussels and cook for 1 minute. Add the shrimp, fish, scallops, and squid and cover the wok. Cook for 3 to 5 minutes; do not overcook. Add the red chilies, cilantro, and scallions. Gently stir to mix in, and serve.

4 steaming

When I was teaching French Techniques at Peter Kump's New York Cooking School, I learned, to my surprise, that students thought of steaming as a technique reserved for health food or vegetarian cuisine; practically the only foods they ever steamed were vegetables. There are without question many healthful aspects to this cooking technique. You do not need to use fats and oils as a cooking medium. When they are added to a dish, it is purely for flavor and, therefore, used in small amounts. Vitamins and minerals are retained, particularly in the case of vegetables. But this is only the beginning of steaming's many virtues. Because steaming cooks by wet heat, food remains moist and tender. And in many preparations, steamed foods can be served directly from the vessel they were cooked in, thus simplifying cleanup. ● In Asia, steaming has been a preferred every-day cooking technique for centuries, and we think nothing of steaming just about any food—whole poultry, fish, seafood, eggs, meats, and simple free-form meat terrines. Even today, full-size ovens are not commonplace in Asian homes, so many foods that westerners would bake are steamed as a matter of course, even breads, buns, and dumplings.

Asians have developed several methods of steaming: (1) food is placed directly on a rack or in a steamer basket set above boiling water, a technique familiar to most cooks; (2) food is placed on a plate, then flavored, sauced, and steamed, plate and all, a technique known as wet steaming; and (3) food is placed in a covered container, which is then placed in a water bath, or bain-marie, a technique that allows food to steam like a plum pudding. The second and third techniques capture all the natural juices and flavors that are otherwise lost during the cooking process. Because water evaporates at 212°F., the heat around the cooking vessel cannot rise above this temperature, so slow and even cooking is ensured.

A wok is indispensable for successful steaming. Its sloping sides easily accommodate a 10-inch steamer basket or rack to hold large pieces of food. With a wok, it is possible to steam foods using only a small amount of water, so none of it spills into your dish and dilutes the flavors. (Should the wok steam dry, simply replenish the water.) Once the food is cooked, you have a built-in warming oven—simply turn off the heat and the dish will stay hot in the covered wok.

Note that when using bamboo steamer baskets *it is not necessary to cover the wok with a lid;* the basket's own lid will trap the steam as it rises. You can also stack several baskets, one on top of the other; as long as the topmost basket is covered, all the food in the baskets below will be bathed in steam.

Stackable steamer baskets are extremely inexpensive, so do invest in a 10-inch one.

Wet steaming lends itself to "cook and serve"—a great labor saver for home entertaining. The soft indirect steam will not damage even the most delicate plates, so use your best china: Place food directly on individual dinner plates, set each plate in a steamer basket, stack the baskets in the wok for steaming, and serve your dinner on the same plate.

Leaves, edible or not, are sometimes used to wrap foods for steaming. Malaysian Otak Otak (page 100) and Steamed Lotus-Wrapped Chicken (page 106) are dishes that use leaf wrappers. In most instances, the leaf is simply a vessel and does not impart any flavor to the food. The exception is the lotus leaf. The subtle aroma of lotus permeates the food in which it is wrapped, and adds another dimension to the dish.

I urge you to steam, steam, steam in your wok—even dishes with French, Italian, and American accents. You will not only enjoy delicious food but will find that you can cut calories and fat without even thinking about it.

vegetables, tofu, and custards

Crisp Broccoli Steamed with Oyster Sauce

In my cooking classes, students never tired of discussing the best way to steam vegetables. They acknowledged that when vegetables are steamed on a rack set directly over water, nutrients are lost. It was easy to convince them that with the Chinese technique of placing vegetables on a plate, flavoring them, and then steaming everything on the plate, all the nutrients and natural juices of the food are retained. This method is obviously better, even if you opt to flavor your vegetables with nothing more than salt and pepper. Any kind of vegetable can be steamed in this way, but here I have chosen ordinary broccoli, which retains its natural sweetness.

SERVES 6

1 pound firm broccoli
¼ cup Basic Chicken Broth (page 22)
2 tablespoons oyster sauce
1 tablespoon thin soy sauce
½ teaspoon freshly ground black pepper
1 teaspoon Asian sesame oil or other flavored oil
1 tablespoon hot red pepper flakes (optional)

Trim the broccoli into spears and remove the stems. Arrange the broccoli spears on a plate that will fit into a steamer basket.

In a small bowl, combine the broth, oyster sauce, soy, black pepper, and sesame oil. Pour the mixture over the broccoli, and put the plate holding the broccoli into a steamer basket. Cover the steamer basket and place in a stainless-steel or coated-aluminum wok with just enough water to reach 2 inches up the sides of the basket. Bring to a simmer over medium heat, and steam for about 10 minutes, or until the broccoli is tender but still crisp. Sprinkle with pepper flakes, if desired, and serve immediately.

Stuffed Cucumbers

I loved this dish when I was a child. It was always served with a white sauce made from stock that was light enough to allow the flavor of cucumber to come through. Sadly, we seldom see cucumbers served as a cooked vegetable these days, but this dish still remains a favorite with me.

SERVES 4

3 cucumbers (about 2 pounds)

For the Filling
½ pound ground pork
2 teaspoons grated peeled fresh ginger
1 tablespoon oyster sauce
1 teaspoon thin soy sauce
½ teaspoon freshly ground white pepper
1 teaspoon cornstarch

For the Sauce
⅔ cup Basic Chicken Broth (page 22) or canned broth
1 tablespoon thin soy sauce
1 teaspoon freshly ground white pepper
1½ teaspoons cornstarch mixed with 2 tablespoons cold water

1 scallion (green parts only), finely minced
2 teaspoons Asian sesame oil

Peel the cucumbers and cut them into 2-inch-thick rounds. With a melon baller, scoop out the seeds completely and discard.

Prepare the filling: In a small bowl, lightly toss together the pork, ginger, oyster sauce, soy sauce, white pepper, and cornstarch to mix well.

Spoon the filling into the centers of the cucumber slices and arrange the rounds on a 9-inch plate. Place the plate in a 10-inch bamboo steamer basket, cover the basket, and set it in a stainless-steel or coated-aluminum wok filled with enough water to reach 2 inches up the sides of the basket. Bring the water to a boil, reduce the heat to medium, and steam the cucumber rounds for 25 to 30 minutes, until the cucumbers are tender but crisp and the filling is cooked.

Meanwhile, prepare the sauce: In a small stainless-steel or coated-aluminum wok, combine the chicken broth, soy sauce, and white pepper. Bring to a boil and add the cornstarch mixture. Continue to simmer for 1 minute, until the sauce thickens. Pour the sauce over the cucumbers, coating them well. Sprinkle with the scallion and sesame oil.

Silken Tofu with Baby Bok Choy

Silken tofu is called for here, but in a pinch the more commonly available soft tofu works just as well. This makes a quick, satisfyingly light lunch when served with rice.

SERVES 2

½ **pound baby bok choy**
½ **pound silken tofu, or soft**
1 **tablespoon oyster sauce**
2 **tablespoons Basic Vegetable Broth (page 17) or Basic Chicken Broth (page 22)**
2 **teaspoons thin soy sauce**
2 **teaspoons dry sherry**
2 **teaspoons Asian sesame oil**
½ **teaspoon chili paste (optional)**

Clean and trim the baby bok choy; do not remove any water that clings to the leaves. Arrange on a plate. Cut the tofu into 1-inch squares and arrange on top of the bok choy.

In a small bowl, mix together the oyster sauce, broth, soy sauce, sherry, sesame oil, and chili paste, if using. Drizzle the sauce over the tofu and bok choy, and place the plate in a steamer basket. Cover the basket and place in a stainless-steel or coated-aluminum wok. Fill the wok with enough water to come just to the bottom of the basket. Bring to a boil, and steam the tofu and bok choy until the leaves are wilted but still green and the stalks are still crunchy. Remove the plate from the basket and serve.

Steamed Savory Egg Custard with Tofu

I love the texture of this delicate dish. For a smooth egg custard, stir the eggs with just one chopstick so that you do not beat air into the mixture. The tofu adds a different dimension to the texture of the eggs. Served with rice, a light soup, and a dish of stir-fried greens, this makes a meal that is easy, delicious, light, and nutritious.

SERVES 4

4 eggs
4 tablespoons Basic Chicken Broth (page 22), canned broth, or
    water that has been boiled and cooled
1 teaspoon thin soy sauce
Salt and freshly ground white pepper to taste
¼ pound soft tofu
2 teaspoons Asian sesame oil
1 scallion (green and white parts), minced

In a small bowl, combine the eggs, broth, soy sauce, salt, and pepper. Stir with a chopstick until the egg yolks are completely broken and the mixture is well blended. Cut the tofu into small cubes, about ¼ inch square.

Lightly grease a shallow 8-inch bowl with a few drops of the sesame oil. Gently pour in the egg mixture, add the tofu cubes (which will sink to the bottom), and sprinkle with the scallion. Place the bowl in a steamer basket, cover the basket, and set it in a stainless-steel or coated-aluminum wok with enough water to reach the bottom of the basket. Bring the water to a gentle simmer and steam the custard for about 20 minutes, or until just set, being sure to keep the heat very low so the custard will stay smooth. Remove from the heat, drizzle with the remaining sesame oil, and serve warm.

Soft Savory Custard Steamed in a Pumpkin

Steamed savory egg custards are a popular part of the Asian menu. They are simple to put together, and most cooks keep eggs on hand to turn into impromptu meals for unexpected guests. You can prepare this custard in a soufflé dish or custard cups, but the flavor imparted by steaming in a "pumpkin dish" is a delightful addition. Because this custard is very soft, I like to serve it as a first course.

SERVES 6

6 small pumpkins (each about 4 inches in diameter)
3 eggs
3 cups Dashi (page 24)
2 tablespoons sake
2 tablespoons thin soy sauce
1 tablespoon grated peeled fresh ginger
½ teaspoon freshly ground white pepper
2 tablespoons minced scallion (green part only)

Cut off the tops of the pumpkins to form lids. Remove all the seeds and stringy parts.

In a bowl, beat the eggs until well blended. Strain through a fine sieve. Add the dashi, sake, soy, ginger, and white pepper, and stir to blend. Pour the mixture into the pumpkins and sprinkle with the scallion greens. Cover with the pumpkin lids. Place the pumpkins in two steamer baskets; stack the baskets and cover. Place them in a stainless-steel or coated-aluminum wok filled with enough water to reach 2 inches up the sides of the bottommost basket. Steam over low heat for 30 minutes, until the custard is set but still soft. Replenish the water in the wok during steaming as needed. Serve the custard in its pumpkin cups.

Steamed Stuffed Duck

Traditionally, this duck would be completely deboned and then stuffed and trussed before steaming. In some recipes it is taken a step further and deep-fried, so the outside is crispy and the inside soft and succulent. I think this last step is much like gilding the lily, for this duck is perfectly delicious just steamed. Here I keep things simple, steaming the duck, bones and all. The only difference is that the duck will be light in color—not a dark mahogany like a roast duck. This dish is nice served with some steamed bok choy drizzled with a little sesame oil.

SERVES 4 TO 6

1 whole duck (about 5 pounds)

For the Stuffing
½ cup glutinous rice
10 dried Chinese black mushrooms
1 cup warm water
1 tablespoon vegetable oil
¼ cup diced bamboo shoots
1 Chinese sausage, diced, or ¼ cup diced ham
¼ cup raw peanuts
2 scallions (green and white parts), minced
2 teaspoons minced peeled fresh ginger
1 tablespoon thin soy sauce
1 tablespoon dry sherry

1 tablespoon dark soy sauce

Trim the duck of any excess fat. Bring a pot of water to a boil and dip the duck into the boiling water for 1 to 2 minutes. Remove the duck and pat dry. Place on a rack to air-dry.

Meanwhile, prepare the stuffing: Soak the glutinous rice in cold water for 1 hour. Soak the mushrooms in the warm water until they are soft; drain, squeezing to remove excess water. Reserve the soaking liquid. Remove and discard the stems from the mushrooms. Cut the mushrooms into ¼-inch dice.

In a carbon-steel wok, heat the oil and add the mushrooms, bamboo shoots, sausage, peanuts, scallions, and ginger. Stir-fry for 1 minute. Drain the rice and add to the wok together with the reserved mushroom soaking liquid, thin soy sauce, and sherry. Cook until the rice has absorbed all the liquid. Remove from the heat and let cool.

When the stuffing has cooled, stuff the duck. Sew up the cavity and truss the duck into a tight ball. Brush the duck all over with the dark soy sauce.

Place a metal rack about 6 inches in diameter inside a stainless-steel or coated-aluminum wok. Place the duck on a plate and then place the plate on the rack. Fill the wok with 3 inches of water, or just until the water barely touches the bottom of the plate. Place a damp dishcloth under the lid of the wok and cover tightly. The cloth will absorb any condensation and prevent the duck juices from becoming diluted.

Steam the duck over moderate heat for 2 hours, or until the duck is very tender and falling off the bone. Be sure to replenish the water in the wok from time to time. Remove the duck on its plate from the steamer basket, and let cool for 10 minutes. Remove the trussing twine and serve the duck directly from the plate on which it was cooked. The duck is so tender that pieces can be picked off by diners, in the Chinese manner, or you can "cut" it into serving portions with a spoon.

Shredded Chicken with Hoisin

I developed this dish for a course on low-fat cooking. Shredding the chicken gives the dish a little more texture. You can also add slivered arrowhead tubers, called *tse goo* in Cantonese, if you see them in an Asian market.

SERVES 4

2 to 3 boneless, skinless chicken breasts (about 2 pounds)
1 cup sliced water chestnuts, preferably fresh
2 garlic cloves, minced
2 teaspoons minced peeled fresh ginger
¼ cup hoisin sauce
1 tablespoon thin soy sauce
1 teaspoon freshly ground black pepper
2 teaspoons cornstarch
2 teaspoons dry sherry
1 tablespoon Asian sesame oil
½ cup cilantro leaves, coarsely chopped

Cut the chicken into strips about ¼ inch wide and 2 inches long.

In a bowl, toss the chicken, water chestnuts, garlic, ginger, hoisin, soy, pepper, cornstarch, sherry, and 2 teaspoons of the sesame oil. Mix well. Add the cilantro leaves and mix well.

Oil a shallow bowl with the remaining sesame oil. Spoon the chicken mixture loosely into the bowl and lightly level off with the back of a spoon; do not pack down. Place the bowl in a bamboo steamer basket; cover the basket and set in a stainless-steel or coated-aluminum wok with enough water to reach 2 inches up the sides of the basket. Steam for 20 minutes, or until the chicken turns white and is cooked through. Serve hot.

meat

Steamed Pork Cake with Dried Scallops

Adding dried scallops, a delicacy in Chinese cooking, to an everyday dish makes it special. This recipe is one my brother-in-law, Michael, makes often for his family. His daughters call it "grapple-hook" cake because of the Chinese gadget he uses for lifting hot plates from the steamer. Do take the trouble to peel fresh water chestnuts for this dish, if you can get them. Their sweet crispness is well worth the effort. You can substitute jicama for the water chestnuts.

SERVES 4

1 cup hot water
¼ teaspoon sugar
⅓ cup dried scallops (about 2 ounces)
½ cup sliced water chestnuts, preferably fresh
1 pound ground pork
1 tablespoon minced peeled fresh ginger
2 scallions (green and white parts), minced
2 teaspoons salt
½ teaspoon freshly ground black pepper
1 teaspoon cornstarch
1 tablespoon Asian sesame oil

In a small bowl, combine the hot water and sugar, stirring to dissolve. Add the scallops and let stand for 15 to 20 minutes, until soft. Drain and shred the scallops very finely with your fingers. Peel the water chestnuts and chop coarsely. In a bowl, toss the pork, scallops, water chestnuts, ginger, scallions, salt, pepper, and cornstarch. Mix well.

Lightly oil a shallow bowl with 1 teaspoon of the sesame oil, and pat the mixture lightly into the bowl. The cake should not be more than 2 inches thick. Place the bowl in a steamer basket. Cover the basket and place in a stainless-steel or coated-aluminum wok with enough water to reach 2 inches up the sides of the basket. Steam for 20 to 25 minutes, or until the pork cake is cooked. Remove the bowl from the basket, drizzle with the remaining sesame oil, and serve.

Steamed Beef Meatballs

For these smooth-textured meatballs, the beef must be ground very, very finely—once a tedious process done with a cleaver. Today, you can accomplish this task in minutes with a food processor. The bitterness of the watercress balances the savoriness of the meat very nicely. This is a popular dim sum item, but when served with a bowl of white steamed rice, it makes a simple dinner.

SERVES 4 TO 5

1 pound ground beef chuck
5 water chestnuts
2 slices peeled fresh ginger (each about the size of quarter)
1 scallion (green and white parts), cut into 2-inch pieces
Zest of 1 orange
1 tablespoon light soy sauce
1 tablespoon plus 1 teaspoon Asian sesame oil
1 teaspoon freshly ground black pepper
2 teaspoons cornstarch
1 egg white
2 bunches of watercress
1 tablespoon salt

In a food processor, combine the beef, water chestnuts, ginger, scallion, orange zest, soy, 1 teaspoon of the sesame oil, the pepper, cornstarch, and egg white. Pulse to a smooth puree.

Fill a large bowl with ice and water, and bring a large pot of water to a boil. Pinch off the leaves of the watercress and discard the stems. Add the salt to the boiling water, then add the watercress. Blanch for just about 5 seconds, until the leaves turn a bright green. Drain immediately and plunge into the ice water. Remove and drain well.

Oil an 8-inch plate with the remaining 1 tablespoon of sesame oil. Arrange the watercress in a layer over the bottom of the plate. With wet hands, form the beef mixture into balls the size of a walnut; you will have about 20 meatballs. Arrange the meatballs on the watercress. Place the plate in a steamer basket. Cover the basket and place it in a stainless-steel or coated-aluminum wok with enough water to come 2 inches up the sides of the basket. Steam for 20 to 25 minutes, until the meatballs are cooked through. Serve them directly from the plate.

fish and seafood

Basic Steamed Fish

The Chinese housewife prefers to buy her fish alive and kicking, and killed to order. Steaming is universally preferred for fish this fresh, and the flavorings would simply be a bit of soy, slivered scallion, and ginger. You can steam any fresh fish this way, including a whole bass, snapper, or salmon, as well as cod steaks and even thin fillets. Steamed flounder, when it is pristinely fresh, is considered elegant enough to be included in any banquet.

When steaming whole fish, the only thing you have to be careful about is the cooking time, which must be tailored to the thickness of the fish. I use 7 minutes to the inch as a rule of thumb for just-done fish fillets; 15 to 20 minutes is a good guideline for whole fish with the bone in. Thin fillets of sole or flounder will steam in as little as 5 minutes.

SERVES 4 TO 6

1 whole flounder (about 10 inches long), cleaned
1 tablespoon thin soy sauce
1 tablespoon finely slivered peeled fresh ginger
1 tablespoon finely slivered scallion (green and white parts)
1 teaspoon vegetable or Asian sesame oil

Rinse the fish and pat dry with paper towels. Lay the fish on a large plate, drizzle with the soy, and sprinkle with the ginger and scallion. Drizzle the oil all over the fish. Place the plate in a steamer basket and cover with the bamboo lid, or place a rack in the wok, set the plate on the rack, and cover tightly with a metal lid lined with a damp cloth. Steam for 7 to 10 minutes, or until the fish begins to flake.

Steamed Fish Steaks

The flavors in this dish are reminiscent of Cambodian cooking. You can increase the amount of bean thread noodles and make this a one-dish noodle meal.

SERVES 4

1 ounce bean thread noodles
1 tablespoon dried shrimp
1 2-inch piece tamarind pulp
¼ cup warm water
1 teaspoon *ketjap manis* (Indonesian sweet soy)
3 Kaffir lime leaves
¼ cup Tamarind Broth (page 18) or Fish and Shrimp Broth (page 24)
4 fish steaks, such as cod, salmon, or Chilean sea bass (each
    about ½ pound and 1 inch thick)
1 tablespoon yellow bean paste
3 garlic cloves, minced
1 tablespoon slivered peeled fresh ginger
1 scallion (green and white parts), cut into 2-inch slivers
1 tablespoon Asian sesame oil
Cilantro sprigs, for garnish (optional)

In a bowl of warm water, soak the bean threads for 15 minutes, or until soft and pliable. Drain and cut into 4-inch pieces, if desired. In another small bowl, soak the dried shrimp in warm water for 15 minutes, or until soft. Drain and coarsely chop. Place the piece of tamarind in the warm water and soak for 15 minutes, or until the pulp breaks up. Remove any seeds or strings, reserving the pulp and soaking liquid.

In a small saucepan, combine the tamarind pulp and soaking water, *ketjap manis,* lime leaves, and broth. Bring to a boil and cook over high heat for 5 to 7 minutes, until reduced by half. Remove the lime leaves and discard them.

Mound the bean threads on a plate that will fit into a steamer basket, and arrange the fish on top of the bean threads. Spread with the bean paste and garlic, then top with the ginger and scallion. Drizzle with the oil and pour the tamarind mixture over the fish. Put the plate in the steamer basket. Cover and place the steamer basket in a stainless-steel or coated-aluminum wok with just enough water to reach 2 inches up the sides of the basket. Steam over medium heat for 10 minutes, or until the fish just flakes. Uncover and garnish with cilantro sprigs, if desired.

Sea Bass Fillet with Yogurt and Indian Spices

Aromatic Indian spices make this quick and easy way with fish delicious. If you like spicy food, you can add a dash of cayenne pepper or top the fish with hot chilies. This dish is nice served with basmati rice steamed with a clove or two, and a simple green vegetable, such as fresh peas or green beans tossed in grainy mustard instead of butter.

SERVES 4

1 sea bass fillet (1½ pounds)
1 teaspoon salt, plus additional for sprinkling
1 teaspoon freshly ground black pepper, plus additional for sprinkling
1 cup nonfat yogurt
Juice of ½ lemon
½ teaspoon ground cumin
½ teaspoon ground cardamom
½ teaspoon ground coriander
¼ teaspoon ground cinnamon
Minced scallion greens or minced hot chilies

Rinse the fish and pat dry with paper towels. Lay the fish on an oiled plate large enough to hold it in one piece, or cut into individual servings. Sprinkle with salt and pepper.

In a bowl, mix together the yogurt, lemon juice, cumin, cardamom, coriander, cinnamon, 1 teaspoon of the salt, and 1 teaspoon of the pepper. Spoon over the fish and spread to coat the fish well. Sprinkle with the scallion greens.

Put the fish plate in a steamer basket; cover the basket and place in a stainless-steel or coated-aluminum wok with enough water to reach 2 inches up the sides of the basket. Steam the fish over medium heat for 20 minutes, or until it is opaque and just done.

Steamed Whole Sea Bass
with Sour Sauce

This is a slightly more elaborate version of Basic Steamed Fish. Unless you have a very large steamer, you must not buy too large a fish—10 to 12 inches is about the maximum length that will fit into most steamers. If you wish to increase the servings, use two fish. They can be steamed on one plate, or on separate plates set in individual baskets and stacked. The sour sauce topping can be made hot and spicy with the addition of cayenne pepper.

SERVES 2 TO 4

1 whole sea bass, scaled and cleaned (about 12 inches long)
3 slices peeled fresh ginger (each about the size of a quarter), slivered
2 scallions (green and white parts), slivered
2 teaspoons thin soy sauce

For the Sauce

1 cup Fish and Shrimp Broth (page 24)
¼ cup dry white wine
1 tablespoon fish sauce (*nuoc mam* or *nam pla*)
1 tablespoon thin soy sauce
3 tablespoons cider vinegar
½ teaspoon sugar
1 tablespoon cornstarch mixed with cold water

2 teaspoons Asian sesame oil
1 scallion, green and white parts, slivered, for garnish

Rinse the fish under cold running water, and pat dry with paper towels. Cut three shallow slashes on the top side of the fish. Place the fish on a plate. Press the ginger and scallions into the cavity of the fish and into the slashes. Drizzle with the soy sauce. Place the plate in a steamer basket; cover the basket and place in a stainless-steel or coated-aluminum wok with enough water to reach 2 inches up the sides of the basket. Steam over medium heat for 20 to 25 minutes, or until the fish turns white and just begins to flake.

Meanwhile, prepare the sauce: In a small wok, combine the broth, wine, fish sauce, soy, vinegar, and sugar. Bring to a simmer and cook for 1 minute. Add the cornstarch mixture, return to a boil, and cook for 1 minute longer, until the sauce thickens.

Pour the sauce over the fish, drizzle with the sesame oil, and sprinkle with the scallion.

Steamed Flower Shrimp

Presentation is what makes this dish. The shrimp are formed to look like flowers, and when they are cooked, they turn a lovely pink, which is set off by the bright green of the vegetables—a contrast that embodies the yin-yang principle in Chinese cooking. Surround your plate with baby bok choy, which will steam with the shrimp, or steam the shrimp on a bed of pea shoot leaves.

SERVES 4

12 jumbo shrimp
1 tablespoon fermented black beans
2 large garlic cloves, minced
1 teaspooon minced peeled fresh ginger
1 tablespoon dry bread crumbs
$\frac{1}{2}$ teaspoon chili paste
1 teaspoon thin soy sauce
1 tablespoon Asian sesame oil
4 heads of baby bok choy or $\frac{1}{2}$ pound pea shoot leaves, tough
  stems discarded

Peel the shrimp, but leave the tail shells on. Cut along the back of each shrimp almost all the way through, remove the vein, and make a small slit in the middle of the shrimp. Curl the tail under toward the middle of the shrimp and push it up through the slit to form a flower shape.

Rinse the black beans in warm water; drain. In a small bowl, mash the beans lightly with the garlic and ginger. Add the bread crumbs, chili paste, soy, and 1 teaspoon of the sesame oil, and mix well. Place about a teaspoon of the mixture on each shrimp just in front of the tail. Press into place.

Arrange the baby bok choy around the outside of the plate, and arrange the shrimp in the center; alternatively, make a bed of pea shoot leaves and arrange the shrimp on top. Drizzle the remaining sesame oil over the shrimp, and place the plate in a steamer basket. Cover the basket and place in a wok with enough water to reach 2 inches up the sides of the basket. Cover tightly and steam over moderate heat for 8 minutes, until the shrimp turn pink.

Steamed Savory Meringue
with Crabmeat

Steaming in the Asian way keeps eggs moist and delicious. Here I use just egg whites mixed with the crabmeat for a delightfully light brunch dish. Prepare the crabmeat mixture in advance and fold in the egg whites at the last minute. Straw mushrooms, which grow in rice paddies, are popular in China, and their mild flavor is perfect for this dish. Unfortunately, we cannot get fresh straw mushrooms in this country, but the canned ones are worth trying. If Chinese celery is available, do use it, as it is much sweeter than regular celery when cooked. Serving this in individual ramekins makes a nice presentation.

SERVES 6

1 8-ounce can straw mushrooms
½ pound fresh lump crabmeat
3 tablespoons unsalted butter
¼ cup finely diced Chinese or regular celery
¼ cup finely diced orange bell pepper
1 tablespoon chopped chives
2 tablespoons minced cilantro leaves
½ teaspoon hot pepper sauce, or to taste
10 egg whites
⅛ teaspoon cream of tartar
¼ teaspoon salt
Orange Miso Vinaigrette (page 182)
Cilantro sprigs, for garnish

Drain the mushrooms and rinse quickly in cold water. Pick over the crabmeat carefully to remove any cartilage or bits of shell. Melt the butter in a small saucepan. With a pastry brush, very lightly butter six 3-inch ramekins.

Pour the remaining butter into a carbon-steel wok. Over medium-low heat, stir-fry the celery and peppers for 2 minutes, or until wilted. Add the mushrooms and cook, stirring, for another minute. Remove the vegetables to a bowl. Add the crabmeat, chives, cilantro leaves, and hot pepper sauce. Toss to mix well. *The mixture may be held in the refrigerator at this point.*

Whisk the egg whites with the cream of tartar until foamy. Add the salt and continue whisking until the egg whites are firm but not dry. With a rubber spatula, stir half the egg whites into the crabmeat mixture. Fold in the remaining egg whites.

Spoon the crabmeat meringue into the ramekins. Place the ramekins in two bamboo steamer baskets. Stack the baskets, cover, and place in a wok filled with enough water to reach 2 inches up the sides of the bottommost basket. Bring to a boil and steam over moderate heat for 10 to 12 minutes, or until the meringue is just set. Remove from the heat and drizzle with a little vinaigrette. Garnish with cilantro sprigs and serve immediately with the remaining vinaigrette.

Scallops Steamed in Sake

Sea scallops are best for this dish. The sweetness of the scallops is enhanced by sake and shiso leaves. Shiso leaves will probably entail a trip to a Japanese market, but if you have a garden or even a pot in a sunny spot, they are amazingly easy to grow. Either the green variety or red leaves will work in this recipe.

SERVES 4

1 pound sea scallops
2 teaspoons white miso
½ cup sake
1 teaspoon salt
½ teaspoon Japanese pepper *(sansho)*
4 shisho leaves, finely shredded

Remove and discard the adductor muscle from the side of each scallop. In a small bowl, mix the miso, sake, salt, and pepper. Place the scallops on a dish and pour the mixture over the scallops. Sprinkle with the shiso leaves.

Place the scallops in a bamboo steamer basket. Cover the basket and place in a stainless-steel or coated-aluminum wok with enough water to come 2 inches up the sides of the basket. Steam over moderate heat for 8 minutes, until the scallops just turn opaque. Remove and serve immediately.

Steamed Mussels in Curry Broth

Mussels are inexpensive and quick to cook, and I've never understood why some people shy away from preparing them. This is an easy and delicious recipe that I hope will convert you to cooking mussels often. Serve them with the broth as a first course, or add crusty bread and a salad for a main dish that will be ready in 30 minutes. If you prefer to keep the broth clear and thin, leave out the heavy cream. Remember when dealing with shellfish to discard any that are cracked or open.

SERVES 8 AS A FIRST COURSE

3 pounds mussels
1 tablespoon vegetable oil
2 medium onions, chopped
1 head of garlic, peeled and crushed
3 tablespoons Red Curry Paste (page 191)
1 teaspoon ground turmeric
2 cups dry white wine
2 cups clam juice
10 Kaffir lime leaves
4 stalks lemongrass (white part only), very thinly sliced
½ cup heavy cream
1 cup (loosely packed) cilantro leaves

With a vegetable brush, clean the mussels under cold running water. Pull off and discard any beards. Discard any mussels with a broken shell or those that do not close when sharply tapped. Drain well.

In a stainless-steel or coated-aluminum wok, heat the oil over medium heat. Add the onions and garlic, and stir-fry until the onion is wilted. Add the curry paste and turmeric, and cook, stirring, for about 1 minute, until aromatic. Add the wine, clam juice, lime leaves, and lemongrass. Bring to a simmer and cook for 5 minutes. Remove the lime leaves and discard.

Add the mussels, cover the wok tightly, and steam over moderate heat for 5 minutes. The mussels will begin to open. Uncover the wok and remove the mussels to a serving bowl as they open. Continue cooking until all the mussels have opened; discard any that fail to open. Add the cream and cilantro leaves to the wok, and stir to blend. Pour over the mussels and serve.

Oyster Mushrooms with Scallops

The oysterlike flavor of these mushrooms makes them a perfect match for scallops, particularly with a touch of oyster sauce to round off the flavors. I like to use butter to bring out the richness of the dish, but you can substitute oil if you wish. Served with white rice, this makes a one-dish meal you'll have ready in 20 minutes.

SERVES 4

½ pound oyster mushrooms
1 pound sea scallops
1 tablespoon oyster sauce
¼ cup Fish and Shrimp Broth (page 24) or Basic Chicken Broth
    (page 22)
¼ teaspoon freshly ground black pepper
1 tablespoon unsalted butter
1 teaspoon minced peeled fresh ginger
1 garlic clove, minced
2 scallions (green and white parts), minced
6 small heads of baby bok choy or mustard cabbage
Salt to taste
1 tablespoon Asian sesame oil

Clean the mushrooms with a damp towel and cut into uniform pieces. Remove the adductor muscle from the scallops, if desired. In a small bowl, combine the oyster sauce, broth, and pepper.

In a carbon-steel wok, melt the butter over medium heat. Add the mushrooms and stir-fry over medium-high heat for 3 minutes, or until the mushrooms are soft and tender. Cool.

Place the scallops on a plate. Pour the mushrooms and any pan juices over the scallops. Drizzle the oyster sauce mixture over the scallops and mushrooms. Sprinkle with the ginger, garlic, and scallions. Place the baby cabbages around the edge of the plate and sprinkle them with salt and the sesame oil.

Place the plate in a bamboo steamer basket. Cover the steamer basket and place in a stainless-steel or coated-aluminum wok filled with enough water to reach 2 inches up the sides of the basket. Bring the water to a boil over medium heat, and steam for 10 to 15 minutes, or until the scallops are opaque and the vegetables are tender but still crisp. Remove the plate from the basket and serve.

dumplings, rolls, and bundles

Wonton Wrapper Dough

Asian markets and many supermarkets now carry fresh wonton and dumpling skins. But as there are many recipes that use wonton wrappers, I have included this recipe for those who want to try their hands at making the wrappers from scratch. The dough may also be used to make fresh noodles, which is an easy job if you have a pasta machine.

MAKES 80 TO 100 WONTON WRAPPERS

1½ **cups all-purpose flour**
½ **cup cornstarch**
2 **eggs**
1 **teaspoon vegetable oil**

In a food processor, combine the flour and cornstarch. Add the eggs and oil, and process just until a ball of dough is formed. Remove to a lightly floured board and knead until smooth. Cover well with a clean cloth and let rest for 30 minutes.

By hand or with a pasta machine (without the "cutters"), roll out the dough to the desired thickness. Cut into 3-inch circles or squares depending on the shape of the dumplings your recipe calls for. Or cut for noodles. To keep wrappers pliable, wrap them well in plastic. Noodles may be dried before using, or kept in a plastic bag.

Wheat Starch Dough

Wheat starch is a by-product of making wheat gluten, an ingredient widely used in vegetarian cooking. A ball of dough is repeatedly washed and the white milky water is evaporated away, leaving a silky white powder, which is the wheat starch. In their typically thrifty way, Asians found a use for this flour. Tapioca flour gives this wrapper its translucence when the dough is cooked. The dough is best worked warm, so if you need more than one recipe, make up only one batch at a time. This dough does not store well; make it and use immediately.

MAKES ENOUGH FOR 36 DUMPLINGS

1 cup wheat starch
½ cup tapioca flour
1 cup boiling water
1 tablespoon oil, plus additional to work with

Combine the wheat starch and tapioca flour in a mixing bowl. Whisk to blend well. In a small saucepan, bring the water to a boil. Add the oil and immediately pour over the flour mixture. Stir with a pair of chopsticks or a fork until the dough forms a ball that holds together.

Oil the work surface and your hands. When the dough is cool enough to handle but still warm, turn it out onto the board and knead for 5 to 10 minutes, or until smooth. Divide the dough into 4 pieces. With a rolling pin, roll each piece into a sausage about ¾ inch across. Cut each sausage into 9 pieces and roll into balls. Roll each ball into a 2½-inch circle. While you work on a piece of dough, keep the other pieces covered with a clean cloth or plastic wrap.

Tofu and Pickled Radish Dumplings

These dumplings are an example of the fusion cooking of Macao, the Portuguese enclave at the mouth of the Pearl River where my family comes from. Although the ingredients are familiar elements of dim sum cuisine, you will not find these dumplings in any dim sum restaurants. We used to have them as part of our Sunday breakfasts after church and at every tea party. The original version contained a little bit of finely shredded pork, which I have omitted to keep this dumpling vegetarian. To make in advance and store, ready for a Sunday brunch, cook the dumplings for 3 to 5 minutes, only to set the dough, then freeze them. To reheat, steam the frozen dumplings.

MAKES 36 DUMPLINGS

For the Filling
1/2 **pound firm tofu**
1/4 **cup finely diced pickled radish**
1 **teaspoon thin soy sauce**
1 **tablespoon finely minced scallion (green and white parts)**
1/4 **teaspoon chili paste with garlic**

Oil to work with
1 **recipe Wheat Starch Dough (page 95)**
Napa cabbage leaves, for lining steamer basket (optional)
Lemon-Chili Soy Dip (page 185)

Prepare the filling: Cut the tofu into tiny cubes, about 1/8 inch square. In a bowl, combine the tofu, pickled radish, soy sauce, scallion, and chili paste. Toss lightly with a fork to mix well.

Oil a board and your hands. Place a scant teaspoon of filling in the middle of each circle and crimp the edges together, gathering them up to form a beggar's purse. Pour a little oil onto a plate and stand the finished dumplings in the oil to grease the bottoms, or line steamer baskets with Napa cabbage leaves and omit oiling the bottoms of the dumplings. Place the dumplings in a steamer basket; cover the basket and place in a stainless-steel or coated-aluminum wok with just enough water to reach the bottom of the basket. Steam for 7 to 10 minutes, or until the dough becomes translucent. Do not oversteam, as the dough will become gluey and sticky. Serve warm with the dipping sauce.

Steamed Lobster Rice Rolls

Rich in lobster meat, these rolls make a filling lunch or first course. The Asian flavorings are light and clean to allow the lobster to dominate. They need only a drizzle of fish sauce mixed with lemon to finish them off. Although you can use fresh rice noodle sheets, which might mean a trip to Chinatown, I prefer the large 9-inch rounds of dry rice paper, which are shelf stable and make a more compact package.

SERVES 4

2 lobsters (each about 1 pound)
2 teaspoons finely slivered peeled fresh ginger
1 tablespoon finely slivered scallion (green and white parts)
1 tablespoon light soy sauce
2 teaspoons sherry
1/4 teaspoon freshly ground black pepper
1 teaspoon cornstarch
4 9-inch round rice paper wrappers

Cook the lobsters in rapidly boiling water for about 10 minutes, or until they turn bright orange. Remove from the water and cool. Crack the shells and remove the meat from the tails and claws. Halve the tails lengthwise and then cut into chunks.

In a bowl, toss the lobster meat with the ginger, scallion, soy, sherry, pepper, and cornstarch.

Dip the rice paper rounds into a bowl of warm water for a few seconds and then lay them on a clean work surface. They will become soft and pliable in a minute. Divide the lobster meat into 4 equal portions and lay each portion on a wrapper. Fold in the sides, then roll up to form a rectangular package.

Place the lobster packages on a plate that fits into a steamer basket. Place the plate in the steamed basket. Cover the basket and place in a stainless-steel or coated-aluminum wok filled with enough water to reach 2 inches up the sides of the basket. Steam the lobster rolls over medium heat for 10 minutes, until they are warmed through. Serve warm or at room temperature.

Garlic Chive and Fish Dumplings

I love these delicious dumplings, which are a variation of the delicate *har kow* shrimp dumplings of classic dim sum cuisine. *Har kow* were always a childhood favorite of mine, and even now I always order them when having dim sum, for they serve as a yardstick of the quality of a restaurant. I have varied the filling by using fish with the garlic chives. If making the dough is too bothersome, use packaged thin wonton skins. They will taste just as good. If you prepare them ahead, it is best to slightly undercook the dumplings made with wheat starch dough and freeze them. Leftover dumplings may be frozen after they are cooked, and reheated without defrosting.

MAKES 36 DUMPLINGS

½ **pound garlic chives**
3 **tablespoons vegetable oil**
1 **tablespoon minced peeled fresh ginger**
2 **teaspoons cornstarch mixed with 2 tablespoons cold water**
½ **pound flounder fillets**
1 **tablespoon thin soy sauce**
1 **teaspoon freshly ground black pepper**
2 **teaspoons dry sherry**
2 **teaspoons Asian sesame oil**
1 **recipe Wheat Starch Dough (page 95) or 1 package of thin round**
     wonton skins
Cabbage leaves, for lining steamer basket
Lemon-Chili Soy Dip (page 185)

Rinse and trim the garlic chives; cut them into 1-inch pieces. In a small carbon-steel wok, heat 1 tablespoon of the vegetable oil and stir-fry the ginger for a few seconds, until aromatic; be careful not to burn the ginger. Add the chives and stir-fry for 30 seconds. Add the cornstarch mixture and cook until thickened, stirring to bind the garlic chives. Remove from the heat and cool.

Check the fish for any bones and remove them with needle-nose pliers. Cut the fish into pieces. In a food processor, pulse the fish until coarsely ground. Add the chive mixture, soy sauce, pepper, sherry, and sesame oil. Pulse to blend well.

Divide the wheat starch dough into 36 walnut-size balls. Use 2 tablespoons of the vegetable oil to grease your hands and the work surface. With a small rolling pin, roll each ball of dough into a thin circle about 2½ inches in diameter. If using wonton skins, lay them out on the work surface, a dozen at a time.

Place 1 teaspoon of the filling in the center of each circle. Lift up half of the circle with your thumb and pleat half of the edge. Press together the pleated edge and the plain edge, and seal to form a crescent-shaped dumpling. Alternatively, pleat the edge of the circle completely and pinch edges together to form a beggar's purse. Leave the dumpling on the work surface while forming it, so the bottom will be flat. Repeat to form 36 dumplings.

Line a bamboo steamer basket with cabbage leaves and place in a stainless-steel or coated-aluminum wok filled with enough water to touch the bottom of the basket. Bring the water to a boil, cover tightly, and steam for 3 to 5 minutes to wilt the cabbage leaves slightly.

Arrange the dumplings on the leaves and steam for 5 to 8 minutes, or until the dumplings become translucent. Serve warm with the dipping sauce.

Chicken and Jicama Filling for Dumplings

Try this filling in your favorite dumpling or wonton recipe for a change of pace. Fill and steam as for Garlic Chive and Fish Dumplings (page 98). Wet your hands with cold water before handling the filling.

MAKES 48 DUMPLINGS

1 pound ground chicken
½ cup peeled and diced jicama
2 teaspoons thin soy sauce
1 teaspoon hoisin sauce
1 teaspoon minced peeled fresh ginger
1 tablespoon cornstarch
1 teaspoon salt
½ teaspoon freshly ground black pepper
1 tablespoon Asian sesame oil
½ cup coarsely chopped cilantro leaves

In a bowl, combine the chicken and jicama. Toss with a fork to blend. Add the soy sauce, hoisin sauce, ginger, cornstarch, salt, pepper, sesame oil, and cilantro leaves. Toss to mix well. Chill slightly before using.

Malaysian Otak Otak

These dumplings have all the sweet and perfumed flavors typical of Malaysia, offset here by the spicy hot chilies. Typically, these leaf packages of fish custard were grilled at the edges of a barbecue, but I like to steam the packages and serve them as hors d'oeuvres. Wrapping food in banana leaves is both practical and pretty—the deep green bundles always elicit applause for their presentation as well as their delicious flavors. Banana leaves are available, frozen, in Asian and Spanish markets. They should be rinsed in warm water before use to remove the powdery film. I tear any leaf too small to use into thin ribbons for tying the bundles. This is an Asian dish, so you will notice the texture of the fish—the filling is not an absolutely silken custard.

MAKES ABOUT 48 PACKETS

1 package of frozen banana leaves
½ pound flounder or cod fillets
1 stalk lemongrass
3 Kaffir lime leaves
3 fresh red chilies
1 garlic clove
1 teaspoon ground turmeric
5 macadamia nuts
1 small onion
1 slice peeled fresh ginger (about the size of a quarter)
1 egg
1 tablespoon tamarind water, made by soaking a 1-inch square of
    tamarind pulp in hot water
½ cup coconut milk
1 teaspoon salt
¼ teaspoon freshly ground black pepper
Pinch of sugar

Soak the banana leaves in a large flat pan of warm water, then rinse and drain. Check the fish to make sure it is free of pin bones; remove any bones with needle-nose pliers. Cut the fish into chunks. Remove and discard the coarse outer leaves of the lemongrass; cut off the tough green parts and discard. Slice the white part of the lemongrass very thinly. Stack the lime leaves, roll up like a cigarette, and cut into a fine julienne.

In the bowl of a food processor, combine the chilies, garlic, turmeric, macadamia nuts, onion, and ginger. Pulse to chop coarsely. Add the fish, egg, tamarind water, coconut milk, salt, black pepper, and sugar. Process until pureed. Remove to a bowl and stir in the lemongrass and lime leaves.

With a pair of scissors, cut the banana leaves into rectangles measuring 3½ inches by 8 inches. Tear an undersized leaf into thin ribbons to tie up the bundles, if desired. Spoon 1 table-spoon of the fish mixture onto one end of each rectangle. Roll up and tie with ribbons or skewer with toothpicks to close. It is not necessary to fold the sides.

Place the bundles in stackable bamboo steamer baskets. Place the baskets in a stainless-steel or coated-aluminum wok filled with just enough water to touch the underside of the bottommost basket. Bring to a boil, reduce the heat, and steam for 10 to 15 minutes, or until the leaf packets feel firm to the touch and the fish is cooked. Remove from the heat, cool slightly, and serve. Packets are unwrapped to be eaten.

Wild Mushroom Buns

Yeast dough buns are the bread of northern China, where wheat rather than rice is the staple crop. When I was growing up in Hong Kong, you could buy these dumplings from street vendors who steamed them on top of coal-filled oil barrels. They were filled with pork and cabbage and were absolutely delicious. Here I use a filling that is earthy and strongly flavored, but these buns can be steamed plain or filled with any kind of filling—pork, vegetables, chicken. Try to roll out the dough as thinly as possible.

I like to steam and freeze these dumplings. To reheat them, I fry the bottoms till golden, then add a tablespoon or two of water to the pan and cover it to steam the tops and heat the filling.

MAKES 30 BUNS

For the Yeast Dough
1 teaspoon dry yeast
1 tablespoon sugar
1 cup warm water
3½ cups all-purpose flour, plus more for the work surface
2 teaspoons salt
1 teaspoon baking powder

For the Filling
¾ pound shiitake mushrooms
¾ pound portobello mushrooms
1 tablespoon light olive oil
1 scallion (green and white parts), minced
2 teaspoons minced peeled fresh ginger
2 garlic cloves, minced
2 tablespoons dry sherry
2 tablespoons oyster sauce
1 tablespoon soy sauce
1 teaspoon sugar
½ teaspoon freshly ground black pepper
Salt to taste

Cabbage leaves, for lining the steamer baskets

Make the dough: Combine the yeast and sugar. Dissolve in the warm water and let stand for 10 minutes to proof the yeast. In a large bowl, mix together the flour and salt. Make a well in the center of the flour and add the yeast mixture. Mix to form a ball of dough. If the dough is too dry, knead in $1/2$ to 1 teaspoon of water. Turn out onto a lightly floured surface and knead for about 20 minutes, or until smooth. Place in an oiled bowl, cover, and let stand in a warm place for about 2 hours, or until the dough has doubled in bulk. The dough is ready when an indentation made with your finger does not spring back.

While the dough is rising, make the filling. Clean the mushrooms with damp paper towels. Remove the shiitake stems and discard. Slice the mushrooms and chop coarsely. In a carbon-steel wok, heat the oil over medium heat. Add the scallion, ginger, and garlic, and stir-fry for 10 seconds, until aromatic. Add the mushrooms and continue cooking until the mushrooms begin to release their juices. Add the sherry, oyster sauce, soy, sugar, and pepper. Stir to blend and continue cooking until the mushrooms are soft and almost completely dry. Salt to taste. Set aside to cool completely.

Punch down the dough and transfer to a floured board. Sprinkle with the baking powder and knead well to incorporate into the dough. Divide the dough into 3 portions. Roll out 1 portion as thinly as possible. Using a 3-inch round cookie cutter, cut 10 circles. Repeat with the remaining dough; you should have 30 circles. Place a teaspoon of filling in the center of each circle. Pleat the edges of the circle and twist tightly to seal. Each bun will look like a beggar's purse. Repeat until all 30 buns are formed. Cover with a clean dishcloth and let stand for 30 minutes to rise again. Place in leaf-lined steamer baskets, twisted-tops up, cover, and place in a stainless-steel or coated-aluminum wok filled with enough water to just touch the underside of the bottommost steamer basket. Cover the top basket and steam over medium heat for about 15 minutes, until the dough puffs up slightly and feels firm like bread. Serve hot.

Seafood Mousse in Crepe Net Bundles

A conversation piece at any dinner party, these beautiful bundles are based on egg net bundles, a classic of the Thai kitchen. The nets take a little practice, but I think the presentation justifies the effort. However, thin crepes will work, if you prefer to use them.

In this recipe, I have made a less eggy crepe batter to set off the flavor of the mousse and reduce the egg content. Salmon and salmon roe make the mousse slightly pink; it peeks through the net, making an intriguing presentation. Serve with a light drizzle of any one of the sauces in chapter 9, or with a beurre blanc flavored with saffron, citrus, or fresh herbs. Even if the fish has been nicely boned, please pass your fingers along the fillet to make sure all the pin bones are removed. Needle-nose pliers make extracting them an easy job.

SERVES 8 AS A FIRST COURSE

¼ **pound salmon fillet, skin and all bones removed**
½ **pound flounder fillet, skin and all bones removed**
½ **pound medium shrimp, shelled and deveined**
1 **tablespoon minced peeled fresh ginger**
2 **tablespoons cornstarch**
1 **tablespoon salt**
1½ **teaspoons freshly ground white pepper**
2 **tablespoons dry white wine**
3 **egg whites**
⅓ **cup heavy cream**
¼ **pound salmon roe**
1 **tablespoon minced chives**

For the Crepe Nets
½ **cup all-purpose flour**
½ **teaspoon salt**
½ **cup low-fat milk**
¼ **cup cold water**
2 **eggs**
2 **tablespoons canola oil**

Vegetable oil, for greasing the skillet
Orange Miso Vinaigrette (page 182) or Kaffir Lime Butter
    (page 186)

Cut the salmon and flounder into large chunks. In a food processor, combine the fish and shrimp. Pulse until coarsely chopped. Add the ginger, cornstarch, salt, pepper, wine, egg whites, and cream. Pulse until smooth. Remove the mixture to a bowl and fold in the salmon roe and chives. Chill.

Meanwhile, make the crepe nets: In a bowl, combine the flour and salt. In a measuring cup, combine the milk, water, and eggs. Beat the eggs to break up, and blend the liquid ingredients well. Make a well in the center of the flour and pour in the liquid, stirring with a whisk to form a smooth batter. Stir in the canola oil and blend well. Let the crepe batter sit for at least 30 minutes. If it is too thick, thin with a little water.

Heat a 10-inch flat skillet over medium heat. Wipe it with a paper towel soaked in vegetable oil. Dip your fingers in the batter and drizzle over the skillet, moving across and back and forth to form a net pattern. Do not make the holes too large. Cook until just set, do not brown. Remove the crepes to paper towels, and stack with wax paper between each crepe. Continue forming crepes until all the batter is used up. You should have 8 crepes.

To assemble: Lay the crepe nets on a work surface. Divide the filling into 8 portions and spoon each portion onto a net, placing the filling slightly off center. Fold once and then fold in the sides. Continue to fold to form a square bundle. Place, seam-side down, on eight 8-inch serving plates.

Place each plate in its own stackable steamer basket. (If you do not have 8 baskets, cook the bundles in batches.) Cover the baskets and place in a stainless-steel or coated-aluminum wok filled with just enough water to touch the underside of the bottommost basket. Steam for about 15 minutes, or until the mousse is set. Remove the plates from the baskets, pour vinaigrette or lime butter around the bundles, and serve.

Steamed Lotus-Wrapped Chicken

I love the lightly perfumed flavor of lotus leaves. This chicken is stuffed with a meaty filling, wrapped in lotus leaves, then steamed until it is falling off the bone and can easily be picked apart with chopsticks.

SERVES 4

4 dried lotus leaves
1 whole chicken (about 3½ pounds)
2 teaspoons vegetable oil
¼ pound ground pork
6 water chestnuts, coarsely chopped
2 tablespoons minced pickled mustard greens (optional)
1 tablespoon minced peeled fresh ginger
2 teaspoons thin soy sauce
½ teaspoon freshly ground black pepper
2 tablespoons dark soy sauce
1 tablespoon dry sherry
2 teaspoons sugar

Rinse the lotus leaves to remove any dust, and soak in warm water for about 15 minutes, or until soft and pliable. Trim the chicken of any excess fat and discard the fat.

Heat the oil in a carbon-steel wok over high heat until just smoking. Add the pork and stir-fry for 1 to 2 minutes. Add the water chestnuts, mustard greens, if using, ginger, thin soy, and pepper. Continue cooking for about 5 minutes, until the pork loses its pink color. Remove from the heat and cool.

In a small bowl, combine the dark soy, sherry, and sugar. Stir to dissolve the sugar. Rub the mixture all over the chicken, inside and out, coating it well. Fill the cavity of the chicken loosely with the pork mixture.

Lay the lotus leaves, overlapping, on a clean work surface. Lay the chicken, breast-side up, in the center of the lotus leaves and fold them over to form a tight package. Tie with twine. Place the chicken on a plate and set in a steamer basket. Place the steamer basket in a stainless-steel or coated-aluminum wok and fill with enough water to reach 2 inches up the sides of the basket. Cover the wok tightly and steam the chicken over medium heat for 2 hours, until very tender. Be sure to replenish the water during the cooking time.

Remove the twine and present the chicken in its wrapping. Cut open the lotus leaves at the table, cut the chicken into serving pieces, and spoon out some of the filling with each portion.

5

poaching

At some point in the '80s, the fish poacher, a handsome (and pricey) elongated pan, became a staple of wedding showers and gourmet kitchens. The lucky owners would poach a whole fish or two—generally salmon, invariably served with a dilled mayonnaise—before relegating the pan to the back of a cabinet. At this point, poaching largely passed out of their kitchen repertoire, save for the odd chicken breast poached for a cold chicken salad. That's a shame, because poaching, the cooking technique in which food is submerged in flavored liquid and gently cooked at a bare simmer is a wonderful way to cook food. Poaching has the advantage of permitting food to retain all its moistness and flavor while rendering some of the fat. Because poached foods, having been cooked with wet heat, do not dry out when cold, as roasted meats do, I like to poach meat, poultry, and seafood, particularly when the dish is to be served at room temperature or cold.

In the Chinese culinary tradition, several techniques fall under the broad definition of poaching, including white poaching and red poaching—two methods defined by the color of the finished food; no-cook poaching, in which the food is not actually cooked but is instead submerged in hot liquid and cooks as the liquid cools; and oil poaching, a self-explanatory technique typical of Chinese cooking and one that I have not encountered in any other cuisine.

White poaching is so named because the flavored poaching liquid adds no color to the food, while red poaching is the term used when the poaching liquid contains dark soy sauce, which gives the cooked food a dark color. In the fanciful Chinese tradition, red describes this technique because it is the color of happiness and good fortune.

I favor no-cook poaching for delicate foods that overcook easily, such as fish, shellfish, and certain vegetables. Oil poaching on the other hand, is ideal for maintaining an ingredient's smooth texture. Nearly all oil-poached dishes are marinated in a mixture of egg white and/or cornstarch to impart a finish known as velveting. Unlike deep-fried food, oil-poached food is never crispy. The oil, which is never heated above 350°F. coats the food being poached, maintaining a velvety texture.

With the exception of oil poaching, poaching generally has the advantage of adding no fat during the cooking process. In fact, much of the fat in the food leeches out into the poaching liquid, making it a great technique for any cooks interested in keeping their dishes low in fat, healthful, and deliciously flavorful.

white-poached dishes

Lo Mein Noodles with Chicken and Yellow Bean Sauce

Lo mein dishes are traditionally stir-fried, but by poaching the chicken strips rather than frying them we are able to keep this quick, easy noodle dish low in fat but still tasty.

SERVES 4 TO 6

½ **pound fresh wheat noodles** *(mein)*
2 **cups Basic Chicken Broth (page 22)**
¾ **pound boneless, skinless chicken breast, cut into strips**
2 **tablespoons minced peeled fresh ginger**
2 **tablespoons yellow bean sauce or white miso**
1 **tablespoon oyster sauce**
2 **tablespoons dry sherry**
1 **tablespoon thin soy sauce**
1 **teaspoon sugar**
1 **tablespoon Asian sesame oil**
3 **tablespoons minced scallions (green and white parts)**
2 **cups bean sprouts**

In a large pot, bring 3 quarts of water to a boil. Add the noodles and cook for 3 to 5 minutes, or until just done. Drain and refresh under cold running water.

In a stainless-steel or coated-aluminum wok, bring the broth to a simmer. Add the chicken strips and gently poach until they turn white. Remove them to a plate.

Return the broth to a simmer and add the ginger, bean sauce, oyster sauce, sherry, soy sauce, and sugar. Stir to mix well. Cook for about 10 minutes, or until the sauce reduces to about 1 cup. Add the chicken to the sauce and stir to mix well. Add the noodles and toss over medium heat just until the noodles are warm. Add the sesame oil, scallions, and bean sprouts. Toss with a pair of tongs to mix well, and serve immediately.

Brined Rolled Turkey Breast

Like most people, I think of turkey as primarily Thanksgiving fare, but this makes a great summer dish. I like to serve this turkey cold, sliced thin and arranged on a bed of lettuce. It is also very good in sandwiches. Brining and then poaching the turkey breast not only gives it more flavor but keeps the meat moist. You can leave the turkey breast on the bone or you can bone, roll, and tie it, which makes it extremely easy to slice.

SERVES 10

3 cups kosher salt
12 cups cold water
3 whole star anise pods
1 tablespoon whole cloves
1 tablespoon fennel seeds
1 tablespoon whole black peppercorns
2 bay leaves
6 slices peeled fresh ginger (each about the size of a quarter)
1 whole turkey breast (about 6 pounds if on the bone or about
    5 pounds if boned and rolled)

In a large stainless-steel or coated-aluminum wok or pot, combine the salt, water, star anise, cloves, fennel seeds, peppercorns, bay leaves, and ginger. Cover the wok and bring the brine to a simmer. Simmer for 15 to 20 minutes, or until the brine is flavored and aromatic. Remove from the heat and cool completely. Submerge the turkey in the brine and let stand for 24 hours.

Remove the turkey from the brine and discard the brine. Fill a wok with 10 cups of fresh cold water. Over high heat, bring the water to a boil, add the turkey, reduce the heat to low, and simmer for 20 minutes. Remove the turkey and discard the water. Add 10 cups of fresh water and poach until the turkey is tender and cooked through, another 25 to 30 minutes if the turkey is on the bone or 15 to 20 minutes if boned and rolled. Cool and serve warm or cold.

Poached Brined Duck

Meats that are salt-cured and then poached are common to many cuisines. This is my version of the Chinese classic that I served, with great success, at the very first Chinese New Year dinner held at the James Beard House. Clove oil is a nice touch to finish the duck. For presentation, you may prefer to skin the duck pieces before serving. Mound the duck on a bed of root vegetables, such as turnips, parsnips, and carrots, which make a nice accompaniment.

SERVES 4 TO 6

3 cups kosher salt
12 cups cold water
3 whole star anise pods
15 cardamom pods
1 tablespoon fennel seeds
1 tablespoon coriander seeds
6 slices peeled fresh ginger (each about the size of a quarter)
1 duck (about 5 to 6 pounds)
Clove Oil (see Variation, page 180)

Measure out 2 tablespoons of the salt and set aside. In a large stainless-steel or coated-aluminum wok or pot, combine the remaining salt, water, star anise, cardamom pods, fennel seeds, coriander seeds, and ginger. Cover the wok and bring the brine to a simmer. Simmer for 15 to 20 minutes, or until the brine is flavored and aromatic. Remove from the heat and cool completely.

Meanwhile, rub the duck with the reserved 2 tablespoons of salt, inside and out. Set on a rack to drain for about 1 hour. Rinse the duck with cold water, pat dry, and truss. Submerge the duck in the cooled brine and let stand for 24 hours.

Remove the duck from the brine, draining well. Fill a large stainless-steel or coated-aluminum wok or pot with 10 to 12 cups of fresh cold water. Over high heat, bring the water to a boil, add the duck, reduce the heat to low, and simmer for 20 minutes. Remove the duck and discard the water. Fill the wok with clean water and bring it to a boil again. Add the duck and simmer for another 20 minutes, or until the duck is tender and cooked through. (Root vegetables may be cooked along with the duck in the second pot of water, if desired.) Cool slightly and cut the duck into serving pieces. Skin, if desired, and brush with clove oil. Arrange on a platter and serve.

Poached Shrimp with Enoki Mushrooms in a Salad

Shrimp poach to a beautiful pink that contrasts nicely with the pencil-thin enoki mushrooms, so this salad is pleasing to the eye as well as the palate.

SERVES 2

7 ounces enoki mushrooms

For the Court Bouillon
½ cup dry white wine
2 cups water
1 bay leaf
1 tablespoon minced shallots
2 to 3 sprigs of fresh thyme

½ pound medium shrimp in their shells

For the Miso Vinaigrette
2 teaspoons white miso
1 teaspoon minced peeled fresh ginger
¼ teaspoon freshly ground white pepper
2½ tablespoons fresh orange juice
1 tablespoon canola oil
1 teaspoon sesame oil
1 teaspoon orange zest

Cut off and discard the ends of the enoki mushrooms.

Prepare the court bouillon: In a stainless-steel or coated-aluminum wok, combine the wine, water, bay leaf, shallots, and thyme. Bring to a boil, reduce the heat, and simmer, covered, for 15 minutes, or until the mixture is aromatic.

Add the shrimp in their shells to the wok, and poach, uncovered, for 5 to 8 minutes, just until they turn pink. Remove them with a slotted spoon and set aside. Strain the bouillon and return the liquid to the wok; discard the herbs.

When the shrimp are cool enough to handle, remove the shells and add them to the bouillon in the wok. Combine the shrimp with the enoki mushrooms and set aside. Simmer the broth for another 15 minutes, then strain it to remove the shells. Discard the shells. Return the liquid to the wok and cook over high heat until it has reduced to 2 tablespoons.

Prepare the miso vinaigrette: In a small bowl, combine the miso, ginger, and pepper. Slowly whisk in the reduced shrimp liquid to smooth out the miso. Add the orange juice and whisk in the canola and sesame oils in a steady stream to form a creamy dressing. Stir in the orange zest. Pour the dressing over the shrimp and enoki mushrooms, and toss to blend well.

Tea-Poached Salmon

Cooking with tea has always intrigued me. When it is used as a poaching liquid, the slight bitterness of tea offsets the rich oily flavor of salmon. It is important that you use dried Chinese orange or tangerine peel *(chenpi)* in the tea, which has a stronger citrus flavor than fresh peel or even home-dried peel. If you choose to remove the skin from the salmon fillet, consider wrapping it in cheesecloth so it is easier to handle without breaking. The cooking time in this recipe will result in a piece of fish that is almost raw at the center, but you can cook it as rare or as well done as you like. Just adjust the time.

SERVES 4

$\frac{1}{3}$ cup tea leaves, such as Assam, orange pekoe, or Darjeeling
$\frac{1}{4}$ cup dried citrus peel *(chenpi)*
1 salmon fillet, completely boned and with skin left on (about
    $2\frac{1}{2}$ pounds)
Ginger-Mustard Mayonnaise (page 187)

Bring 1 quart of water to a rolling boil. Warm a teapot or glass measuring cup and pour in the tea leaves. Pour the boiling water over the tea leaves, cover, and let steep for 5 minutes. You will have a very strong tea. Strain the tea into a large stainless-steel or coated-aluminum wok. Add about another quart of hot water to the tea, then add the citrus peel. Return to a simmer and cook for 3 minutes. Add the salmon and poach the fish for 15 to 18 minutes, until it just begins to flake. Do not overcook. Remove the fish to a platter and serve warm or cold with ginger-mustard mayonnaise.

red-poached dishes

Red-Poached Squab

Squab, considered a delicacy and a special treat, is very popular with Asians. You will find it is always available in Chinatown markets, where it is more reasonably priced than at fancy butcher shops. Use this same liquid, with your own variations to the herbal mix, to poach any poultry: chicken, duck, game hens, or even little quail. In some instances, especially when the poultry has a high fat content like duck, you may want to dunk the bird in hot water before poaching.

MAKES 4 APPETIZERS

2 squab (each about 1 pound)
1½ cups dark soy sauce
1 cassia bark or cinnamon stick (about 3 inches long)
1 teaspoon five-spice powder
1 tablespoon sugar
1 slice of fresh ginger (about the size of a quarter)
1 scallion
2 tablespoons Asian sesame oil
Shredded lettuce or wilted greens (optional)

With a long piece of butcher's twine, truss the squab: tie the legs together and tie the wings, so the birds form compact packages and will cook evenly.

In a stainless-steel or coated-aluminum wok, combine the soy sauce, cassia bark, five-spice powder, sugar, ginger, and scallion with enough water to cover the squab completely. Cover the wok and bring the liquid to a boil, then reduce the heat and simmer the liquid for 15 minutes, or until it is aromatic.

Add the squab to the poaching liquid and return to a simmer. Poach the squab for 10 to 15 minutes, or until just done. Remove from the heat and cool. Rub the squab all over with the sesame oil, cut into quarters, and serve on a bed of shredded lettuce.

Red-Poached Duck

This is a classic of the cooking of Chiu Chow. Although goose is the preferred bird, I am using duck, which is more readily available. Don't forgo the dunking in hot water. This step cleanses some of the surface fat and enables the soy to penetrate better, making for a beautiful mahogany bird. Paint it with a little flavored oil, usually sesame, but flavored Clove Oil (see Variation, page 180) is a nice innovation. Unless you have a king-size wok, this is one time when a deep pot will work better.

SERVES 6

1 duck (about 6 pounds)
2 cups dark soy sauce
1 cassia bark or cinnamon stick (about 3 inches long)
1 tablespoon whole star anise pods
1 tablespoon fennel seeds
2 teaspoons whole cloves
2 slices peeled fresh ginger (each about the size of a quarter)
2 scallions
¼ cup honey
10 to 12 cups water
Asian sesame oil or Clove Oil (page 180)

Bring a large pot of water to a boil. Turn off the heat and immediately dunk the duck into the water, then remove and pat dry with paper towels. Place the duck on a rack to air-dry while you prepare the poaching liquid.

In a large stainless-steel or coated-aluminum wok or a deep pot, combine the soy sauce, cassia bark, star anise, fennel seeds, cloves, ginger, scallions, honey, and water. Bring to a boil, cover, and simmer for 15 minutes, until the liquid is aromatic.

Add the duck to the poaching liquid, pushing down to submerge it completely. Return to a boil, reduce the heat, and simmer for 1½ to 2 hours, or until the juices run clear when the duck is pricked at the thigh. Remove the duck to a platter, let it cool, and then brush with the sesame oil. Cut into pieces and serve warm or at room temperature.

Red-Poached Filet Mignon

This poached filet of beef beats any oven-roasted filet for juiciness and tenderness, particularly when it is served cold. It has been a best-seller in my catering repertoire since I started the business 20 years ago. I like this beef best really rare, or *bleu* as the French say, but it will not be dry even if you cook it to medium. The dark soy, a hallmark of red poaching in Chinese cooking, gives the beef a nice brown color, which makes it look so appetizing. Leftovers are delicious in any main dish salad that calls for roasted or grilled beef. If the filet is too long to fit comfortably in your wok, cut it in half and poach both pieces at the same time.

SERVES 8 TO 10

1 whole filet mignon (about 4 to 5 pounds)
1 cup dark soy sauce
½ cup thin soy sauce
½ cup whole star anise pods
¼ cup Szechwan peppercorns
1 tablespoon fennel seeds
2 cinnamon sticks
2 slices peeled fresh ginger (each about the size of a quarter)
2 whole scallions (green and white parts)

Trim the beef of all fat. Turn the thin tail end over so the filet is of uniform thickness, and tie securely. (You can have the butcher do this for you.)

In a wok, combine the two soy sauces, star anise, Szechwan peppercorns, fennel seeds, cinnamon sticks, ginger, and scallions with enough water to just cover the beef when submerged, about 8 cups. Bring to a simmer and cook, covered, for 10 to 15 minutes, until the liquid is aromatic.

Add the beef to the poaching liquid and cook at a gentle simmer. For rare, cook for 25 to 30 minutes, or until the internal temperature reaches 110 to 115°F.; for medium rare, cook another 5 to 10 minutes to 120°F. Remove the meat from the liquid and let stand for at least 20 minutes before serving; the internal temperature will rise another 10 degrees as it stands.

Red-Poached Lamb

You will need a large wok to poach this lamb, but the strips should fit nicely. Although I'm not usually partial to cold lamb, this richly flavored recipe is an exception. It stays moist and delicious, and I like to use it in main-dish salads. Have the butcher cut the strips of lamb from a boneless leg.

SERVES 4 TO 6

2 cups dark soy sauce
½ cup thin soy sauce
¼ cup dry sherry
2 tablespoons Szechwan peppercorns
3 whole star anise pods
2 slices peeled fresh ginger (each about the size of a quarter)
2 whole scallions
2 dried hot chilies, left whole
1 tablespoon sugar
3 pounds boneless lamb, cut into strips about 2 inches thick

In a large stainless-steel or coated-aluminum wok, combine the two soy sauces, sherry, Szechwan peppercorns, star anise, ginger, scallions, chilies, and sugar with about 8 cups of water. Cover the wok. Bring the liquid to a boil, then reduce the heat and simmer for 15 minutes, or until the liquid is aromatic.

Slide the lamb strips gently down the sides of the wok and poach at a gentle simmer for 15 minutes, until the lamb is cooked but still pink inside. Remove from the poaching liquid and let stand for at least 15 minutes. Serve warm or at room temperature.

"no-cook" poached dishes

No-Cook Poached Chicken and Two Chicken Salads

This is a old Chinese trick for poaching chicken that you will love, especially on those dog days of summer when no one can stand the heat in the kitchen. The chicken is actually "cooked" in the retained heat of the poaching liquid, so not only does the chef keep cool, but the chicken retains all its natural juices and stays deliciously moist. Even though I use Asian flavorings in this recipe, you can flavor the poaching water with any combination of herbs and vegetables, even the classic French mirepoix and bouquet garni. Placing metal spoons inside the chicken before cooking ensures good heat conduction. In the old days, we were exhorted to use only silver spoons, but ordinary stainless ones work just fine.

SERVES 4

1 whole chicken (about 3 pounds)
2 slices peeled fresh ginger (each about the size of a quarter)
2 whole scallions
1 tablespoon Szechwan peppercorns

Remove any excess fat from the chicken. Place two metal teaspoons in the cavity of the chicken.

In a large stainless-steel or coated-aluminum wok, place enough water to cover the chicken completely. Add the ginger, scallions, and Szechwan peppercorns. Bring to a boil, reduce the heat to low, and simmer, covered, for 10 to 15 minutes, until the poaching liquid is aromatic. Add the chicken and push it down so it is completely covered by the liquid. Return the liquid to a boil and immediately turn off the heat and cover the pot. Let the chicken cool in the poaching liquid for at least 1 hour, or longer, then remove from the liquid and cool to room temperature. Cut the chicken into bite-size pieces and serve with any of the dipping sauces from chapter 9 or use in salads.

Chicken Noodle Salad with Thai Basil Dressing

This chicken salad is a delicious way to use no-cook chicken. Served on a bed of rice stick noodles, the salad makes an easy main meal, one that is particularly nice in warm weather. The Thai basil gives it a special flavor, but in a pinch you can use any other basil, though the flavor will be a little different.

SERVES 2

½ **pound rice stick noodles**
1 **whole poached chicken breast (about** ½ **pound)**

For the Dressing
2 **tablespoons chunky peanut butter**
½ **cup unsweetened coconut milk**
1 **garlic clove, finely minced**
2 **teaspoons (packed) brown sugar**
1 **tablespoon fish sauce** (*nuoc nam* or *nam pla*)
½ **teaspoon chili oil**
1 **tablespoon fresh lemon or lime juice**

½ **cup (loosely packed) Thai basil leaves, coarsely torn**

Soak the rice stick noodles in very hot water for about 20 minutes, until soft. Drain well and set aside. Shred the cooked chicken with your fingers, or cut into a fine dice.

Prepare the dressing: In a small mixing bowl, slowly whisk together the peanut butter and coconut milk until smooth. Add the garlic, brown sugar, fish sauce, and chili oil. Whisk until the sugar is dissolved and the mixture is well blended. Add the lemon or lime juice and stir to blend.

In a bowl, toss the chicken with half of the dressing and then toss in the basil leaves and mix to blend well. In another bowl, toss the noodles with the remaining dressing. Arrange the noodles on a serving platter or individual plates. Top the noodles with the chicken salad and serve.

Sesame Chicken Salad

On hot summer days when the thought of cooking in a hot kitchen puts even *me* off, my thoughts turn to chicken salad. The ever popular flavors of the sesame dressing will make this salad special. Make an extra batch of the dressing and have it ready to toss into a salad for another day. It will keep a week or longer, refrigerated.

SERVES 4

2 cups shredded poached skinless chicken (white and dark meat)
1 cup diced Granny Smith apple, tossed in lemon juice

For the Dressing
3 garlic cloves, peeled
1 tablespoon minced peeled fresh ginger
1 tablespoon minced shallot
2 tablespoons sesame paste or chunky peanut butter
1 tablespoon honey
3 tablespoons warm water
1 tablespoon dark soy sauce
3 tablespoons rice vinegar
3 tablespoons Asian sesame oil
2 teaspoons salt
1 teaspoon freshly ground black pepper

¼ cup cashews, coarsely chopped
1 tablespoon minced scallion (green part only)

In a bowl, toss the shredded chicken and apples together.

Prepare the dressing: In a blender or food processor, mince the garlic, then add the ginger, shallot, sesame paste, honey, water, soy, vinegar, sesame oil, salt, and pepper. Process until a smooth sauce is formed.

Pour the sauce over the chicken mixture and toss to coat well. Add the nuts and scallion, and toss to mix.

No-Cook Poached Fish Slices
with Spicy Wine Sauce

I first learned this technique from James Beard, who recommended it for cooking asparagus, and I found it especially useful on catering jobs. I later realized that this method worked perfectly with fish fillets when I had to poach fish to serve one hundred. If your wok does not have a lid, heavy-duty aluminum foil will do fine—just be sure to cover the fish immediately after the boiling water is poured on.

SERVES 4

1 fish fillet (about 1 pound), such as bass or mahimahi, skinned and boned
2 tablespoons cornstarch
2 teaspoons salt
1 teaspoon freshly ground white pepper

For the Sauce
½ cup dry white wine
1 tablespoon dark soy sauce
½ teaspoon cayenne
½ teaspoon sugar
¼ teaspoon salt
¾ cup Basic Chicken Broth (page 22) mixed with 1½ tablespoons cornstarch
1 tablespoon Asian sesame oil

1 scallion (green and white parts), julienned
3 tablespoons vegetable oil

Cut the fillet into pieces, about 2 inches square. Mix the cornstarch with the salt and white pepper, spread on a piece of wax paper, and coat the fish pieces.

Arrange the fish in a single layer in a wok. Bring a kettle of water to a boil. Pour enough boiling water over the fish to cover by 1 inch, then immediately cover with a lid or foil and let stand for 10 to 12 minutes. The fish will poach as the water cools, and it will not overcook. The fish can be left in the water to keep warm.

Meanwhile, make the sauce: In a wok or small saucepan, combine the white wine, soy, cayenne, sugar, salt, and broth mixture. Bring to a simmer and cook for about 1 minute, until thickened. Add the sesame oil.

With a slotted spoon, remove the fish to a serving platter. Sprinkle with the scallion. Heat the vegetable oil until just smoking and pour over the fish. Immediately pour the sauce over the fish and serve.

oil-poached dishes

Oil-Poached Jade Chicken

In my view, velveting chicken is one of the great techniques of Chinese cooking. While you will find recipes that call for poaching the chicken mixture in water, I believe that too much of the smooth, velvety texture is lost in water poaching and the only way to go is oil poaching. The snow peas need just a quick pass through the oil to remove the raw taste and brighten the green while retaining crispness.

SERVES 4

1 pound boneless, skinless chicken breast
1 egg white
2 teaspoons cornstarch
1 teaspoon salt
¼ pound snow peas, trimmed
3 cups vegetable oil
2 teaspoons minced peeled fresh ginger
1 scallion (white and green parts), minced
1 tablespoon dry sherry
2 teaspoons thin soy sauce
¼ cup Basic Chicken Broth (page 22) mixed with 1 teaspoon
    cornstarch

Cut the chicken into cubes about ½ inch square. In a bowl, combine the egg white, cornstarch, and salt. Add the chicken and toss to coat well. Let stand for at least 10 minutes.

In a carbon-steel wok set over medium-low heat, heat the oil to 350°F. Pass the snow peas through the hot oil with a mesh skimmer or strainer. Do not let them stand in the oil for more than a few seconds, and remove as soon as their color brightens. Drain on paper towels.

Add the chicken to the oil and poach for about 5 minutes, or until the chicken turns white and opaque. Remove and drain on paper towels. Pour off the oil, wipe out the wok with paper towels, and return to the heat.

When the wok is just smoking, add the ginger, scallion, sherry, soy sauce, and broth. Cook just until the mixture thickens, add the chicken and snow peas, toss to coat well, and serve.

Oil-Poached Fish with Black Vinegar

The special flavor of Chinese black vinegar, delicate but distinctive, is a perfect balance for the smooth oil-poached fish. You will enjoy using black vinegar in many dishes, so do seek it out.

SERVES 4

1 pound fish fillet (about 1 pound), such as bass or cod, skinned and boned
2 egg whites
2 teaspoons cornstarch
1 teaspoon salt
3 cups vegetable oil

For the Sauce
¼ cup julienned peeled fresh ginger
1 tablespoon water
¼ cup black vinegar
2 teaspoons thin soy sauce
2 teaspoons Asian sesame oil

1 scallion (green and white parts), julienned

Slice the fish on a slant to obtain pieces 1 inch wide and ½ inch thick. In a bowl, combine the egg whites, cornstarch, and salt. Add the fish pieces and toss to coat well.

In a carbon-steel wok, heat the oil over low to medium heat to 350°F. Add the fish and poach for about 1 minute, just until the fish turns opaque. Remove with a slotted spoon and drain on paper towels. Pour off the oil and wipe out the wok with paper towels.

Prepare the sauce: Return the wok to the heat, add the ginger, water, black vinegar, thin soy sauce, and sesame oil. Bring to a boil, reduce the heat, and simmer for 1 minute.

Transfer the fish to a platter, sprinkle with the scallion, and pour the sauce over the fish just before serving.

Oil-Poached Shrimp with Dragon Well Tea Leaves and Chilies

Use only Dragon Well or Lung Ching tea leaves from Hangzhou for this outstanding dish, as the tea leaves, an essential ingredient, are actually eaten, and only a little of the brewed tea is used. As with all green teas, this special green tea is only tatched, that is, it is simply put in a wok and rolled and roasted over low heat. The tender green leaves have a silken feel and rustle like paper. The very best grade, Lark's Tongue, is not even rolled but consists of tiny leaves that lie flat to dry. The rich sweet taste of the oil-poached shrimp is balanced in this dish by the slight bitterness of the tea leaves. Spicy hot chilies give an added dimension, but you may leave them out if you wish. I like to serve the shrimp in tiny demitasse cups for a very elegant presentation.

SERVES 4

2 egg whites
1 tablespoon plus 1½ teaspoons cornstarch
1 teaspoon salt
1 pound large shrimp, peeled and deveined
2 tablespoons Dragon Well tea leaves
3 cups vegetable oil
1 tablespoon whole dried hot chilies
2 tablespoons dry sherry
Pinch of sugar
Salt to taste

In a bowl, combine the egg whites, 1 tablespoon of the cornstarch, and the salt. Add the shrimp and stir to coat well. Cover and let stand for at least 1 hour and up to 3 days in the refrigerator.

Bring a kettle of water to a boil, warm a teapot or glass measuring cup, and add the tea to the pot. Pour 1 cup of the rapidly boiling water over the tea leaves, cover, and steep for 5 minutes. Drain off the tea, reserving the tea leaves and ½ cup of the brewed tea. Let the tea cool.

Heat the oil in a carbon-steel wok to 350°F. over low to medium heat. Add the shrimp and poach until they just turn pink. Remove with a slotted spoon and drain on paper towels. Add the chilies and poach for 1 minute in the hot oil. Remove the chilies and drain on paper towels. Pour off the oil and discard. Wipe the wok with paper towels.

Mix the cooled ½ cup of tea with the remaining 1½ teaspoons of cornstarch. Return the wok to the heat and add the sherry, sugar, and tea mixture. Cook over medium heat until thickened, then add the tea leaves, shrimp, and chilies and toss to blend and heat through. Season with salt to taste, and serve.

Oil-Poached Pork with Spicy Sauce

This dish illustrates well the yin-yang balance of flavors aimed for in Chinese cooking. The pork slices are smooth, velvety, and simple tasting and contrast well with the pungent spicy sauce.

SERVES 4

1 pound pork tenderloin
2 egg whites
2 teaspoons cornstarch
1/2 teaspoon salt
3 cups vegetable oil
1 small red bell pepper, seeded and diced
2 jalapeños, seeded and sliced
1 teaspoon minced peeled fresh ginger
2 garlic cloves, minced
2 tablespoons fish sauce (*nuoc mam* or *nam pla*)
1/4 cup water
Juice of 1 lime

Cut the pork into 1/4-inch-thick slices. In a bowl, combine the egg whites, cornstarch, and salt. Add the pork slices and toss to coat well. Let stand for about 10 minutes.

In a carbon-steel wok, heat the oil to 350°F. over low to medium heat. With a wire mesh strainer or slotted spoon, pass the red pepper through the hot oil just until slightly softened; do not let the pepper stand in the oil for longer than 10 seconds. Remove and drain on paper towels. Working in 2 batches, add the pork to the oil and poach for 3 minutes, until just cooked. Remove and drain on paper towels. Pour off the oil, strain, cool, and store for reuse or discard. Wipe the wok with paper towels and return the wok to the heat.

When the wok just begins to smoke, add the red pepper, jalapeño slices, ginger, garlic, fish sauce, and water. Toss to mix, then add the pork slices and stir to mix well. Drizzle in the lime juice and serve.

Oil-Poached Scallops with Garlic Slices and Garlic Chives

These quickly poached scallops are just lightly tossed with the poached garlic and garlic chives, and flavored with nothing more than a bit of sherry and salt. The important thing is the smooth texture that is achieved by this method of cooking. The sweetness of the scallops remains uncompromised. If yellow chives are available, try them for a nice change.

SERVES 4

1 pound sea scallops
2 egg whites
2 teaspoons cornstarch
3 cups vegetable oil
12 garlic cloves, thinly sliced
6 ounces garlic chives, cut into 1-inch-long pieces
2 tablespoons dry sherry
¼ cup Fish and Shrimp Broth (page 24) or water
1 teaspoon salt
Pinch of sugar

Remove the tough adductor muscles from the scallops. In a small bowl, combine the egg whites and cornstarch. Add the scallops and toss to mix.

In a carbon-steel wok, heat the oil to 350°F. over low to medium heat. With a slotted spoon or wire mesh strainer, pass the garlic slices through the oil for no longer than 30 seconds, until they barely color. Drain on paper towels. Pass the garlic chives through the oil for about 5 seconds, just until they turn a bright green and begin to wilt. Drain on paper towels.

Gently add the scallops to the oil and poach for 3 to 5 minutes, or until they just turn opaque. Remove with a slotted spoon or wire mesh strainer, and drain well on paper towels. Pour off the hot oil and wipe the wok with paper towels. Return the wok to the heat. Add the scallops, garlic, chives, sherry, broth, salt, and sugar to the hot wok. Toss for 1 minute, or until heated through and well mixed. Serve immediately.

6

stir-frying

Stir-frying, for most people, is synonomous with wok cooking. At some point stir-frying became associated with heavy, oily dishes and fell out of favor. But a well-seasoned carbon-steel wok eventually becomes so smooth that it is virtually nonstick, obviating the need to use large quantities of oil. In fact, I have used as little as a teaspoon of fat to stir-fry a dish that serves four people generously. Greasy dishes are indicative of a failure to use the proper wok and the chef's lack of expertise; they are not a given of stir-frying. ● There are, of course, hundreds, if not thousands, of recipes for stir-fried dishes, and nearly as many books (including one of my own) cover them in depth. Here I offer a few of my special favorites, chosen because they are all easy to prepare. To me, and to most Asians, the stir-fry is Asian fast food, so my recipes contain few labor-intensive steps, such as shredding and fine chopping of ingredients.

Most of the recipes in this chapter are meant to serve four people, with steamed rice as a base. If you wish to serve more people, simply increase the number of dishes for more "tastes." I have included several noodle dishes because they are essentially stir-fries, so use them as your guide and try topping different noodles with your own stir-fried creations. There is one stir-fried rice dish, Nasi Goreng (page 131), but you can vary the ingredients to produce any version of stir-fried rice you like; just remember, you must start with cold cooked rice.

There are few tricks to successful stir-frying but a couple things to keep in mind. For tips on cooking over high heat, refer to these guidelines. As everything happens in minutes and even seconds, premix all the sauce ingredients in one bowl so they can be added to the dish instantly. If you find that you would like a thicker sauce, do not hesitate to thicken it with a slurry made of 1 part cornstarch and 2 parts cold water. This light slurry, used sparingly, will never overthicken your sauce. And, finally, for those of you who imagine you must stir-fry as fast as those speedy TV wok chefs—remember, you can slow everything down to suit your own pace just by turning the heat down a little and cooking your food in smaller batches.

Cook all the recipes in this chapter at least once, and with that experience under your belt, create your own dishes to stir-fry in the wok. You will find it easy and fun, and I know you, too, will become a devotee of Asian fast food.

rice and noodle stir-fries

Lobster *Lo Mein*

I recently had this dish at Noodletown in New York's Chinatown. If you are familiar with classic Chinese cooking, you will recognize this dish, minus the noodles, as lobster cantonese. Use fresh wheat noodles *(mein)* if you can, ideally the flat linguine-shaped kind. If you can't get Chinese noodles, any fresh linguine makes a good substitute.

The lobster is served in the Chinese manner with its shell, and the meat is picked out by the diners, who will agree it is well worth the work. If you are squeamish about killing the lobsters, have the fishmonger do this for you.

SERVES 6

2 live lobsters (each about 1½ to 2 pounds)
2 tablespoons vegetable oil
1 tablespoon minced peeled fresh ginger
¼ cup Shaoshing or dry white wine
2 cups water
1 pound fresh wheat noodles
¼ cup minced scallions (green and white parts)
2 garlic cloves, minced
½ pound finely ground pork

Kill the lobsters. Separate the tails and claws from the bodies, and, with a cleaver, cut into bite-size pieces. In a carbon-steel wok, heat 1 tablespoon of the oil over medium-high heat; add 1 teaspoon of the ginger and the meaty lobster pieces. Stir-fry until the lobster turns red. Add the wine and cook for 1 to 2 minutes longer. Remove the lobster pieces to a plate and keep warm. Add the heads, any shell pieces, and water to the wok, and simmer for 10 to 15 minutes, or until the broth is flavorful. Remove the lobster heads and discard any other shell bits. Skim the broth and reserve.

Meanwhile, bring a pot of water to a rapid boil and cook the noodles until just done. Drain.

In a carbon-steel wok, heat the remaining oil and ginger over medium-high heat. Add 3 tablespoons of the scallions and the garlic, and stir-fry for 30 seconds. Add the pork and cook, breaking up, until the meat loses its pink color. Add the reserved broth, noodles, and lobster pieces, and cook until the noodles have absorbed nearly all the liquid, tossing all the while to mix well. Scatter the remaining scallions over the top and serve.

Pad Thai: Stir-Fried Thai Rice Stick Noodles

There are probably as many versions of pad thai, the traditional Thai noodle dish, as there are cooks, so feel free to play with this version and put your own stamp on it.

SERVES 4 TO 6

1 pound flat rice stick noodles, linguine size
4 eggs
1 tablespoon tomato paste
1 tablespoon sugar
¼ cup fish sauce (*nuoc mam* or *nam pla*)
2 tablespoons vegetable oil
8 garlic cloves, minced
2 cilantro plants (leaves and roots), well washed and minced
1 pound medium shrimp, peeled and deveined
1 cup bean sprouts
¼ cup minced scallions
2 limes, cut in half

For the Garnish
1 tablespoon dried shrimp, ground to a powder
1 tablespoon dried red pepper flakes
¼ cup peanuts, coarsely chopped
1 cup bean sprouts
¼ cup cilantro leaves, coarsely chopped
2 limes, thinly sliced

Soak the rice noodles in a bowl of hot water for 20 minutes, or until soft and opaque. Drain and set aside. In another small bowl, beat the eggs with the tomato paste until well mixed. Stir in the sugar and fish sauce.

In a carbon-steel wok, heat half the oil over high heat until just smoking. Add the garlic and cilantro, and stir-fry for 30 seconds. Add the shrimp, and cook for 1 to 2 minutes, or until the shrimp are just pink. Remove to a plate. Add the egg mixture to the wok and cook, stirring to scramble the eggs. Remove to another plate. Add the remaining oil and the noodles to the wok and cook, spreading the noodles to cook evenly until they soften. Return the shrimp and the egg mixture to the pan. Add the bean sprouts and minced scallions, toss to mix, and squeeze the limes over the noodles. Toss again and mound on a serving platter.

To garnish, sprinkle with the shrimp powder, red pepper flakes, peanuts, bean sprouts, and cilantro leaves, and surround with the lime slices.

Nasi Goreng: Indonesian Fried Rice

Here is fried rice with a twist. Try it and I am sure you will add this delicious dish to your everyday menus. I use poached chicken and shrimp, and "fry" the rice in broth to reduce the fat in this recipe. If you have only raw chicken and shrimp, simply stir-fry them until they are done, before adding the remaining ingredients. A teaspoon of turmeric gives the rice a festive yellow color.

SERVES 6

2 teaspoons vegetable oil
3 eggs, beaten
3 garlic cloves, minced
2 teaspoons shrimp paste
2 teaspoons dried red pepper flakes
1 cup minced onion
1 cup poached chicken breast, cut into cubes
1 cup cooked medium shrimp
3 cups cold cooked rice
1 teaspoon ground turmeric (optional)
1 tablespoon sweet soy sauce *(ketjap manis)*
2 tablespoons chicken broth or water
Salt to taste

Saturate a piece of paper towel with a bit of the vegetable oil. Heat a carbon-steel wok over medium heat until just smoking and wipe with the paper towel. Pour a thin layer of the eggs into the wok and make a crepelike omelet. Transfer to a plate and repeat to use up all the eggs. There will be 3 or 4 crepes, depending on how thin they are. Roll up the egg crepes and cut into narrow ribbons.

With a mortar and pestle, pound together the garlic, shrimp paste, red pepper flakes, and 2 tablespoons of the minced onion until you have a paste. Alternatively, process in a blender until pureed.

In a carbon-steel wok, heat the remaining oil over medium-high heat until just smoking. Add the remaining minced onion and the paste mixture, and fry for about 30 seconds, until aromatic. Add the chicken and shrimp, and fry for 1 minute, stirring to mix; then add the rice, turmeric, if using, sweet soy sauce, and broth. Cook until the rice is hot, tossing to mix well. Season to taste with salt and remove to a serving platter. Scatter the egg ribbons over the top of the rice.

Two Kinds of Noodles with Tree Ears and Chicken

This noodle dish is unusual because it combines rice stick noodles with bean thread, or cellophane, noodles. Bean threads are seldom used as noodles, except in Korean cooking. They are more commonly considered an ingredient for stir-fries and soups. This dish features tree ears, which are considered good for the heart and go particularly well with mushrooms. If you cannot find garlic chives, leave them out and add an equal amount of scallion greens.

SERVES 6

¼ cup dried tree ears
8 dried Chinese black mushrooms
½ pound bean threads
¼ pound rice stick noodles
½ pound boneless, skinless chicken breast
2 teaspoons thin soy sauce
2 teaspoons cornstarch

For the Sauce
½ cup oyster sauce
1 teaspoon thin soy sauce
½ cup Basic Chicken Broth (page 22)
½ teaspoon freshly ground black pepper
2 teaspoons Asian sesame oil

2 tablespoons vegetable oil
4 ounces garlic chives, cut into 2-inch pieces
1 carrot, peeled and cut into matchsticks
1 scallion (green and white parts), cut into 2-inch pieces
2 slices peeled fresh ginger (each about the size of a quarter), slivered

In separate bowls, soak the tree ears, mushrooms, bean threads, and rice sticks in warm water for 15 to 30 minutes, or until all are soft. Drain the tree ears, bean threads, and rice sticks, and discard the water. Drain the mushrooms and reserve the soaking liquid. Coarsely chop the tree ears. Remove and discard the stems from the mushrooms. Cut the mushrooms into shreds.

Cut the chicken into thin slices and marinate in the soy sauce and cornstarch. Let stand for 10 minutes.

Meanwhile, prepare the sauce: In a small bowl, combine the oyster sauce, soy sauce, reserved mushroom liquid, broth, pepper, and sesame oil.

In a carbon-steel wok, over medium heat, heat 1 tablespoon of the vegetable oil. Add the chicken and stir-fry for about 5 minutes, until it just turns white; remove to a plate. Add the remaining vegetable oil to the wok, then add the garlic chives, carrot, scallion, and ginger. Stir-fry for about 1 minute, until wilted. Add the tree ears and mushrooms, and toss to mix well. Add the sauce mixture, chicken, bean threads, and rice stick noodles. Using a pair of tongs, toss to mix well. Bring the sauce to a simmer and cook until the noodles absorb most of the sauce but remain moist.

Crispy Noodle Nests

These noodle nests are very typical of Cantonese-style noodles. The outside is crisp while the inside remains soft. You can make one large pancakelike nest or individual small ones as I've done here. Top them with any of your own favorite stir-fried dishes.

MAKES 6 NESTS

2 tablespoons salt
½ pound very thin fresh wheat noodles *(mein)* or angel hair pasta
3 tablespoons vegetable oil

Bring a large pot of water to a rolling boil; add the salt and noodles. Cook until the noodles are just done. Drain and refresh under cold running water. Drain well again and divide into 6 portions.

In a carbon-steel wok, heat 2 tablespoons of the oil over high heat until just smoking. Gently form 3 circular noodle piles in the wok and press down lightly with a spatula. Cook over medium heat until the bottoms are light brown; turn and continue cooking until the other side is crisp and brown. Remove to paper towels to drain. Repeat with the remaining oil and noodles.

Crumbled Tofu and Scrambled Eggs

Here is a novel way to add protein to your scrambled eggs, making this a hearty dish for lunch or brunch. Fresh chives give it a nice light oniony flavor. Serve the eggs with buttered toast points for an untraditional breakfast.

SERVES 6

½ **pound firm tofu**
6 eggs
1 teaspoon salt
½ **teaspoon freshly ground black pepper**
2 tablespoons minced chives, plus additional for garnish
2 tablespoons butter
1 teaspoon vegetable oil

Place the tofu on a flat plate and mash with a potato masher or heavy fork until crumbled. In a bowl, beat the eggs until well blended. Flavor with salt and pepper, and stir in 2 tablespoons of the chives. Stir in the crumbled tofu.

In a carbon-steel wok, heat the butter and oil over low heat. Add the egg mixture to the wok and cook, stirring constantly, until the eggs are just set. Garnish with chives and serve.

Tea-Smoked Tofu with Wild Mushrooms

The smokiness and slight bitterness of smoked tofu contrasts well with the earthiness of wild mushrooms to give this simple vegetarian dish a nice meaty flavor. Tree ears provide a further textural element, making the dish more interesting to the palate.

SERVES 4

1 tablespoon dried tree ears
6 dried Chinese black mushrooms
¼ pound fresh shiitake mushrooms
¼ pound fresh oyster mushrooms
1 pound Smoked Tofu (page 165)
1 tablespoon vegetable oil
1 tablespoon minced peeled fresh ginger
1 tablespoon minced shallots
2 garlic cloves, minced
¼ cup oyster sauce
1 tablespoon thin soy sauce
2 tablespoons dry sherry
1 tablespoon sesame oil
1 scallion (green and white parts), minced

Place the tree ears and dried mushrooms in separate bowls and pour ⅓ cup of hot water over each. Let stand for 10 to 15 minutes, until soft. Remove the tree ears from the water, rinse in cold water, and cut into uniform bite-size pieces. Remove the mushrooms from the water and reserve the soaking liquid. Cut the fresh mushrooms into bite-size pieces if necessary. Cut the tofu into 1-inch squares.

In a carbon-steel wok, heat the vegetable oil over medium heat; add the ginger, shallots, and garlic, and stir-fry for about 30 seconds to 1 minute, until the shallots are wilted. Add all the mushrooms and tree ears, and stir-fry, tossing frequently, until wilted. Add the tofu, the reserved mushroom liquid, oyster sauce, soy sauce, and sherry. Bring to a simmer and cook for 1 to 2 minutes, tossing to mix well. Sprinkle with the sesame oil and scallion, and serve.

Spicy Orange Chicken Slices

So many of us choose to eat chicken several times a week, and we are always seeking new ways to prepare it. I decided to make this favorite stir-fry with sliced chicken instead of the usual beef. I know this will become a dish you cook often.

SERVES 4

1 pound boneless, skinless chicken breasts

For the Marinade
2 teaspoons dark soy sauce
2 teaspoons dry sherry
1 teaspoon vegetable oil
1 teaspoon minced peeled fresh ginger
1 teaspoon grated orange zest
2 teaspoons cornstarch
½ teaspoon salt
½ teaspoon freshly ground black pepper

For the Sauce
½ cup fresh orange juice
1 tablespoon thin soy sauce
1 tablespoon oyster sauce
1 tablespoon Asian sesame oil
Zest of 1 orange
2 teaspoons sugar
1 teaspoon cornstarch
¼ cup water

¼ cup vegetable oil
2 tablespoons slivered ginger
4 dried hot chilies, crumbled

Cut the chicken breasts into ¼-inch slices.

In a bowl, combine the marinade ingredients: the dark soy sauce, sherry, vegetable oil, ginger, grated orange zest, cornstarch, salt, and pepper. Add the chicken, toss to combine, then let stand for 10 minutes.

In another bowl, combine the sauce ingredients: the orange juice, thin soy sauce, oyster sauce, sesame oil, orange zest, sugar, cornstarch, and water. Whisk to blend well, and set aside.

In a carbon-steel wok, heat the vegetable oil over high heat and stir-fry the chicken in batches for 3 to 5 minutes, until the meat is cooked through. Remove to a plate. Pour off and discard any excess oil, leaving about 1 teaspoon in the wok. Return the wok to the heat, add the ginger slivers and hot chilies, and stir-fry for 30 seconds. Add the chicken and sauce mixture. Bring to a simmer and cook for 3 to 5 minutes, until the sauce thickens. Toss to coat the chicken slices well. Serve immediately.

Lemongrass Chicken

Usually this is made with a whole chicken cut into serving pieces. I prefer to use boneless thighs, but you can use chicken breasts if you like white meat. In either case, I would advise you to leave the skin on, as this keeps the chicken juicier.

SERVES 4

1½ pounds boneless chicken thighs, with skin left on
4 stalks lemongrass
2 teaspoons vegetable oil
3 garlic cloves, crushed
3 scallions (green and white parts), minced
3 fresh red chilies, seeded and minced
2 tablespoons fish sauce *(nuoc mam or nam pla)*
1 teaspoon freshly ground black pepper
1 teaspoon sugar
¼ cup water
½ cup chopped peanuts

Cut the chicken into bite-size pieces. Remove any coarse outer leaves from the lemongrass. Cut off and discard the green tops. Slice the white parts of the stalks as thinly as possible.

In a carbon-steel wok, heat the oil over high heat until just smoking. Add the chicken pieces and brown lightly, turning once or twice. Add the lemongrass, garlic, scallions, and chilies. Stir-fry for 30 seconds, tossing to mix well. Add the fish sauce, black pepper, sugar, and water. Bring to a simmer, and cook for about 15 to 20 minutes, until the chicken is tender and the sauce is syrupy; stir occasionally. Adjust seasonings if necessary, sprinkle with the peanuts, and serve.

Minced Squab in Lettuce Packages

This rich, luxurious dish is often served at banquets. In most recipes, the squab is combined with some ground pork, but this version is unadulterated for a truly sumptuous dish sure to please squab lovers. Don't be daunted by the task of removing the squab from the bones—the meat does not have to remain in nice, whole pieces, since it is going to be minced.

SERVES 4 TO 6

4 whole squab (each about 1 pound)
¼ cup thin soy sauce
¼ cup dry white wine
2 tablespoons Asian sesame oil
6 dried Chinese black mushrooms
1 tablespoon tree ears
1 cup fresh water chestnuts, peeled, or canned, drained and rinsed
¼ cup squab stock or Basic Chicken Broth (page 22)
1 teaspoon sugar
3 tablespoons vegetable oil
2 scallions (green and white parts), minced
1 tablespoon minced fresh ginger
2 teaspoons cornstarch mixed with 1 tablespoon cold water
1 teaspoon freshly ground pepper
Salt to taste
Boston lettuce leaves, for packages
Hoisin sauce

Remove the squab meat from the bones. Use the carcasses for stock, if desired. Remove the skin and cut the meat into chunks. Place the squab meat in a food processor and pulse until coarsely chopped. In a bowl, combine the squab with 2 tablespoons of the soy sauce, 2 tablespoons of the wine, and 1 tablespoon of the sesame oil.

In another bowl, soak the dried mushrooms in ½ cup of hot water for 10 to 15 minutes, until soft. Remove the mushrooms and reserve the soaking liquid. Remove and discard the stems, and cut the mushrooms into fine strips. In another small bowl, soak the tree ears in hot water until soft. Remove, rinse in cold water, and coarsely chop. Coarsely chop the water chestnuts.

In another small bowl, combine the stock, the remaining soy sauce, wine, and sesame oil, and the sugar. Set aside.

In a carbon-steel wok, heat the vegetable oil over high heat until just smoking. Stir-fry the scallions and ginger for about 30 seconds, until aromatic. Add the squab and stir-fry until the meat loses its pink color. Add the mushrooms, tree ears, and water chestnuts, and stir-fry for 1 minute. Add the soy-wine mixture and stir to blend well. Add the cornstarch mixture, bring to a boil, and cook for about 1 minute, until the sauce thickens and binds the squab. Add the pepper and season with salt. Remove to a serving bowl. Serve with a platter of lettuce leaves, so diners can fill leaves with a portion of the squab and roll them to form packages. Pass the hoisin sauce on the side.

Duck with Young Pink Ginger

When ginger is young, before any skin has had a chance to form, it is ivory colored with pink tinges and it need not be peeled. It is juicy and more pungent than regular gingerroot. You can find young ginger in the late spring and early fall. This is the best ginger to pickle for eating with sushi, and it is simply delicious in this dish. You can substitute regular ginger if you must, but in that case, be sure to peel the ginger and soak it in warm water for about 5 minutes.

SERVES 4

1 whole duck breast, bones and skin removed
2 teaspoons thin soy sauce
2 teaspoons cornstarch
$\frac{1}{2}$ teaspoon freshly ground black pepper
$\frac{1}{4}$ cup water
2 tablespoons vegetable oil
1 garlic clove, minced
1 scallion (green and white parts), minced
$\frac{1}{4}$ cup fresh young ginger, cut into $\frac{1}{4}$-inch cubes
$1\frac{1}{2}$ tablespoons yellow bean paste
3 tablespoons dry sherry
1 teaspoon sugar
2 teaspoons Asian sesame oil

Slice the duck into thin pieces about 1 inch long and $\frac{1}{4}$ inch thick. In a small bowl, combine the soy sauce, cornstarch, and pepper. Add the duck to this marinade and mix well; let stand for 10 minutes. Remove the duck and set aside. Add the water to the marinade remaining in the bowl and reserve.

In a carbon-steel wok, heat the vegetable oil over high heat until just smoking, and stir-fry the garlic and scallion for about 30 seconds, until aromatic. Add the duck and stir-fry for about 5 minutes, or until the meat loses its pink color. Add the ginger and toss to mix well. Add the bean paste, sherry, sugar, and marinade. Bring to a simmer and cook for 2 minutes, tossing to blend well. Remove from the heat and drizzle with the sesame oil before serving.

meat stir-fries

Curried Minced Beef with Jicama

Everyone loves dishes made with ground beef, and this simple stir-fry is a sure winner. The flavors are those commonly used in Malaysia, and the coconut milk, besides being delicious, makes the beef extra tender. Serve this dish with white rice.

SERVES 4

1 tablespoon vegetable oil
1 medium onion, minced
2 garlic cloves, minced
1 tablespoon Madras-style curry powder
1 teaspoon ground turmeric
1 pound lean ground beef
1 cup coconut milk
1 cup peeled jicama dice
Salt and freshly ground black pepper to taste

In a carbon-steel wok, heat the oil over high heat until just smoking. Add the onion and garlic, and stir-fry for about 30 seconds, until aromatic. Add the curry powder and turmeric, and stir-fry for 10 seconds. Add the beef and stir-fry, breaking up, for 5 to 7 minutes, until the meat just loses its pink color. Add the coconut milk and bring to a simmer. Add the jicama and stir to mix well. Cook over medium heat for 5 to 7 minutes, until the curry thickens. Season with salt and pepper to taste.

Pork Slices in Hoisin Sauce

When I tell my students to think of hoisin sauce as Chinese ketchup, they instantly grasp its possibilities. This sweet sauce is just as popular in China as ketchup is throughout this country, and those who particularly like its flavor can never get enough of it. This recipe combines sweet hoisin, sweet red and green peppers, and sweet pork—a fortuitous marriage.

SERVES 4 TO 6

1½ pounds pork tenderloin (2 whole tenderloins)

For the Marinade
2 tablespoons dark soy sauce
2 tablespoons dry sherry
1 tablespoon cornstarch

2 tablespoons vegetable oil
4 scallions (green and white parts), minced
1 tablespoon minced peeled fresh ginger
1 green bell pepper, seeded and diced
1 red bell pepper, seeded and diced
¼ cup hoisin sauce
¼ cup dry sherry
Pinch of salt
2 teaspoons freshly ground black pepper
1 tablespoon Asian sesame oil

Slice the pork tenderloin into ¼-inch-thick pieces. In a bowl, combine the marinade ingredients: the dark soy sauce, sherry, and cornstarch. Add the pork and mix; let stand for at least 10 minutes.

In a carbon-steel wok, heat the vegetable oil over high heat until just smoking. Add the scallions and ginger, and stir-fry for about 30 seconds, until aromatic. Add the pork, reserving any remaining marinade, and stir-fry for about 5 minutes, until the pork is just done. Add the green and red peppers, and stir-fry for another minute. Add the hoisin sauce, sherry, salt, and black pepper, and combine. Add 2 tablespoons of water to the marinade remaining in the bowl and add to the wok. Toss to blend well. Remove from the heat, drizzle with the sesame oil, and serve immediately.

seafood stir-fries

Bay Scallops with Shiso Ribbons

The delicate sweetness of bay scallops goes perfectly with shiso's faint anise flavor. I use sake in this dish, but for an East-West touch, try a bit of Pernod. Serve these scallops with white rice.

SERVES 4

1 pound bay scallops
1 tablespoon thin soy sauce
4 teaspoons cornstarch
1/2 teaspoon freshly ground white pepper
5 large shiso leaves
1/4 cup sake
1 tablespoon white miso
1 teaspoon sugar
2 tablespoons vegetable oil
1 teaspoon minced peeled fresh ginger
Salt to taste
1 tablespoon cold water

Remove the tough adductor muscle from the scallops. In a bowl, combine the soy sauce, 2 teaspoons of the cornstarch, and pepper. Add the scallops and toss to coat well; set aside for 5 to 10 minutes. Stack the shiso leaves and cut into thin ribbons. In another small bowl, combine the sake, miso, and sugar. Stir to blend.

In a carbon-steel wok, heat the oil over high heat until just smoking. Add the ginger and stir-fry for 10 seconds. Add the scallops and stir-fry for about 30 seconds, until just opaque. Stir in the shiso ribbons. Add the sake-miso mixture. Make a sherry with 2 teaspoons of the cornstarch and the cold water, and stir it in. Cook for about 1 minute, until thickened. Season with salt to taste.

Shrimp Cantonese

Everyone knows the famous dish lobster cantonese. This version is made with shrimp, which is more readily available and easier on the budget. Of course, lobster still works well and can easily be substituted for the shrimp. Serve this dish with white rice.

SERVES 4

1¼ pounds large shrimp

Marinade for the Shrimp
2 teaspoons thin soy sauce
1 teaspoon vegetable oil
2 teaspoons minced peeled fresh ginger

Marinade for the Pork
1 teaspoon thin soy sauce
1 teaspoon cornstarch
½ teaspoon freshly ground black pepper

¼ pound ground pork
2 tablespoons vegetable oil
1 tablespoon minced peeled fresh ginger
1 scallion (green and white parts), minced
2 tablespoons dry sherry
2 teaspoons thin soy sauce
⅓ cup Basic Chicken Broth (page 22)
½ teaspoon freshly ground black pepper
2 teaspoons cornstarch mixed with 2 tablespoons water
1 tablespoon Asian sesame oil

Shell and devein the shrimp. Rinse them in cold water and pat dry on paper towels. In a bowl, combine the shrimp marinade ingredients: the soy sauce, oil, and ginger. Add the shrimp to the marinade and let stand for at least 15 minutes or overnight in the refrigerator. In another small bowl, combine the pork marinade ingredients: the soy sauce, cornstarch, and pepper. Add the ground pork to the marinade and let stand for 10 minutes.

In a carbon-steel wok, heat the oil over high heat. Add the ginger and scallion, and stir-fry for 30 seconds. Add the shrimp and stir-fry until the shrimp just turn pink. Remove to a plate and keep warm. Add the pork to the wok and stir-fry, breaking up the meat until there are no lumps, cook until the pork loses its pink color. Add the sherry, soy, broth, and pepper. Add the cornstarch mixture and stir to mix in. Bring to a boil, and cook for 1 minute, until the sauce thickens. Return the shrimp to the wok and toss to coat well. Drizzle with the sesame oil.

Tamarind Shrimp

The tart flavor of tamarind goes well with the sweetness of shrimp, which is intensified by the mirin in the dish. This is a quick and easy recipe, and the shrimp need to be marinated for only a short time.

SERVES 4

1 pound large shrimp
2 tablespoons tamarind pulp dissolved in ¼ cup hot water
1 tablespoon thin soy sauce
2 teaspoons minced peeled fresh ginger
3 garlic cloves, minced
2 tablespoons mirin
1 tablespoon Asian sesame oil
1 teaspoon chili paste
1 tablespoon vegetable oil
1 tablespoon minced cilantro leaves

Peel and devein the shrimp. Rinse them in cold water and drain well.

In a bowl, combine the tamarind pulp and water with the soy sauce, 1 teaspoon of the ginger, half the garlic, and the mirin, sesame oil, and chili paste. Add the shrimp, toss, and let stand for 10 minutes.

Remove the shrimp from the marinade; drain them well and reserve the marinade. In a carbon-steel wok, heat the oil over high heat, add the remaining ginger and garlic, and stir-fry for 30 seconds. Add the shrimp and stir-fry until they turn pink and are just done. Add the reserved marinade and cook for another 30 seconds to 1 minute, tossing constantly. Stir in the cilantro, remove from heat, and serve.

7

deep-frying

Cooks know that despite protestations of dietary concerns, no one can resist deliciously crisp fried food. But deep-frying intimidates many cooks. If you are among them, you'll find frying in a wok is a whole new ball game. ● As with stir-frying, the best wok to use is one made of carbon-steel because its light weight conducts heat quickly and efficiently. Its shape and sloping sides allow you to fry with a minimum amount of oil; when I deep-fry in my wok, I rarely have to use more than 2 cups. Oil in small quantities heats up quicker and then there is less to dispose of—so you need not feel guilty about wasting a large amount of oil. The wide opening of the wok allows you to slide food into the oil gently and avoid splatters, and it easily accommodates large items of food, such as a whole fish. ● There are, of course, a few points to bear in mind. First, make sure that your wok is firmly set on the heat source. You can use a flat-bottomed wok or a wok ring stand; or you can invert the grate over the gas burner so that it cradles the wok. Have near the stove a pan lined with paper towels to drain the cooked food. And also have handy a wire mesh strainer and long-handled spatulas and tongs. If you are adept at using them, a pair of long wooden chopsticks are wonderful for lifting single items, like wontons or fritters, out of the hot oil as they brown.

When food is deep-fried, the outside develops a crisp coating while the inside stays moist. It is important that the oil is heated to a minimum temperature of 400°F. when the food first enters the oil. If the oil is too cold, it will be absorbed before a crisp outer coating forms, which can make the food oily and unappetizing. Batters and coatings are aids to getting a crunchy crust, so they should not be allowed to become soggy from sitting too long before they are cooked. After the crust has formed, the heat can be turned down if the item, such as a large fish, needs a longer time to cook through and the outside begins to get too brown.

There is a continuing debate about the kind of oil to use for deep-frying. Peanut oil is often recommended because of its high smoking point. This oil has a very nutty flavor, so unless a dish calls for it, I prefer to use vegetable oil or light olive oil instead. Olive oil has a high smoking point as well, and light olive oil has the added advantages of being inexpensive and not having a strong fruity flavor that might interfere with the taste of the food. For me, the ideal deep-frying oil should not contribute a flavor; it should only be the medium in which the food fries up crisp and crunchy.

Many recipes call for pouring off hot oil. Be very careful when you do this, as an accidental spillage can cause serious burns. I recommend placing a metal or heatproof glass bowl on several layers of paper. Grip the wok firmly by the handles with both hands (well shielded with mitts) and then pour, standing well back to avoid splatters. Do not attempt to strain or discard the oil until it is completely cool. When pouring off deep-frying oil and then reusing the wok, do not wipe out the wok. The residue is enough to stir-fry the ingredients necessary for the sauce, and this way you keep the fat calories at a minimum.

Once you've mastered the art of deep-frying, you may find this guilty pleasure taking a more prominent place at your kitchen table—and only you need know how easy it was!

vegetables and tofu

Vegetable Tempura

Here is my recipe for the best tempura mix ever. It is quick, easy, stretchable, and economical. I have suggested a mix of exotic Asian vegetables, but you can use anything you like or have on hand—bell peppers, eggplant, onions, and even seafood. This amount of batter will make enough tempura for a dozen or more people and can be halved if you like. The amount of water varies because the batter will thicken as it sits and you will have to keep thinning it out. Begin with a ratio of water to flour and cornstarch of at least $1\frac{1}{2}$:1.

SERVES 8

For the Batter
1 cup all-purpose flour
1 cup cornstarch
Ice water
Salt to taste
A few ice cubes

1 piece lotus root (about ¾ pound)
1 sweet potato (about 1 pound)
1 jicama (about 2 pounds)
6 long beans
2 bunches of scallions
3 to 4 cups vegetable oil
Thin soy sauce and vinegar, combined to taste, for a dip

Prepare the batter: In a bowl, combine the flour and cornstarch. Make a well in the center and slowly whisk in enough ice water to form a batter with the consistency of heavy cream. Add salt to taste and two or three ice cubes. The batter will thicken as it stands, but you can keep thinning it with more ice water.

Cut the lotus root, sweet potato, jicama, and long beans into slices, sticks, or chunky pieces as desired. Cut the scallions into pieces about 3 inches long, using both the green and white parts. In a carbon-steel wok, heat the oil over high heat until just smoking. Dunk the vegetables in the batter, a few pieces at a time, and using your hands, drop them into the hot oil. When crisp and golden, remove the tempura pieces with a wire mesh strainer or slotted spoon and drain on paper towels. Mound on a platter and serve with a simple soy and vinegar dip.

Filled Tofu Triangles with Oyster Sauce

Once tofu is deep-fried, it develops a firmer texture, which is very satisfying to meat lovers. These triangles filled with pork are a particularly filling treat.

SERVES 4

6 squares firm tofu

For the Filling
2 scallions (green and white parts), minced
1 slice peeled fresh ginger (about the size of a quarter), minced
1 shallot, minced
1 garlic clove, minced
1 tablespoon cilantro leaves, coarsely chopped
½ pound ground pork
1 tablespoon thin soy sauce
1 tablespoon Asian sesame oil
½ teaspoon freshly ground white pepper
1 tablespoon cornstarch
1 tablespoon dry sherry
¼ teaspoon salt

2 cups vegetable oil

For the Sauce
2 teaspoons minced peeled fresh ginger
2 scallions (white and green parts), minced
2 teaspoons Szechwan peppercorns, ground
2 tablespoons oyster sauce
1 tablespoon thin soy sauce
½ cup water
½ teaspoon sugar

Cut the tofu squares diagonally in half to form 12 triangles. With a knife, make a slit about 1 inch long on the cut edge of each triangle. Scoop out some of the tofu to make a pocket in each triangle.

Prepare the filling: In a small bowl, combine the scallions, ginger, shallot, garlic, cilantro, and pork, and mix well to blend. Add the soy sauce, sesame oil, white pepper, cornstarch, sherry, and salt, and mix in well.

Divide the mixture into 12 portions and fill the tofu triangles.

In a carbon-steel wok, heat the vegetable oil over medium-high heat until just smoking. Gently slide in the tofu triangles and deep-fry until golden, turning once or twice. Remove them to paper towels to drain. Pour off and discard the oil; or let it cool, then strain and reserve for another use. Do not clean the wok.

Prepare the sauce: Return the wok to the heat. Add the ginger, scallions, and Szechwan peppercorns, and stir-fry for 30 seconds, or until aromatic. Add the oyster sauce, soy sauce, water, and sugar. Bring to a simmer and cook for 1 minute.

Return the tofu triangles to the wok and simmer in the sauce to heat through, turning to coat.

Blistered Long Beans

Ordinary green beans can be substituted for Chinese long beans.

SERVES 4 TO 6

1 pound long beans
½ pound ground pork
2 teaspoons dark soy sauce
1 teaspoon cornstarch, plus 2 teaspoons mixed with 3 tablespoons
    cold water
2 cups vegetable oil
4 garlic cloves, minced
1 tablespoon minced peeled fresh ginger
3 scallions (green and white parts), minced
3 dried hot red peppers, crumbled
2 teaspoons Szechwan peppercorns, coarsely crushed
½ cup Basic Chicken Broth (page 22), Basic Vegetable Broth
    (page 17), or water
Salt and freshly ground black pepper to taste
1 tablespoon Asian sesame oil

Rinse the long beans and cut into 2-inch lengths. Dry well. In a small bowl, combine the pork with the soy sauce and 1 teaspoon of the cornstarch, and mix well.

In a carbon-steel wok, heat the oil over medium-high heat until just smoking. In batches, deep-fry the long beans for 5 to 8 minutes, until blistered. Remove to paper towels and drain. When all the beans are fried, pour off the oil. Do not clean the wok.

Return the wok to the heat and add the garlic, ginger, and scallions. Stir-fry for 30 seconds, or until aromatic. Add the pork mixture and stir-fry until the meat loses its pink color, breaking it up as it cooks. Add the hot red peppers, Szechwan peppercorns, and broth. Bring to a simmer and cook for 1 minute. Season with salt and black pepper to taste. Add the cornstarch-and-water mixture, and cook for another minute, until the sauce thickens. Return the long beans to the wok and drizzle in the sesame oil. Toss to blend and heat through.

The Best Chicken Wings Ever

I couldn't resist including this recipe. The wings are so good because they are deep-fried in olive oil. They are quick and simple to prepare, and stay crisp even after they cool, so they are the perfect nibble to put out for a party. I generally just serve them with a bottled blue cheese dressing to which I add hot sauce and a little more crumbled blue cheese.

MAKES 36 WINGS; SERVES 8 TO 10

18 chicken wings, cut in 2 pieces
1 tablespoon salt
1 teaspoon freshly ground black pepper
2 teaspoons ground cumin
2 teaspoons paprika
2 cups light olive oil or pure olive oil

Trim the drummettes if necessary and pat dry with paper towels. In a small bowl, combine the salt, pepper, cumin, and paprika.

In a carbon-steel wok, heat the oil over high heat until just smoking. Sprinkle a few wings at a time with the salt mixture, then slide the flavored wings into the oil. Deep-fry them until light brown and crisp, then remove them from the wok and drain on paper towels. Repeat for the remaining wings. Serve hot, warm, or at room temperature.

Crisp-Fried Poussins

This classic Chinese technique for obtaining a crispy deep-fried bird is the same as that used for the famous Peking duck. You can apply it to chicken, game hens, squab, or any bird you want to deep-fry. The end result more than justifies the long drying time. Try it once and I know you will agree. Serve this bird just by itself or with Anise Pepper Salt (page 180) or Garlic Spice Salt (page 179) for dipping.

MAKES 4 APPETIZERS

2 poussins (each about 1 pound)
8 cups cold water
½ cup honey
2 star anise pods
2 teaspoons salt
2 tablespoons dark soy sauce
½ teaspoon five-spice powder
3 cups vegetable oil
Pea shoots or other greens, for garnish

Remove any innards from the poussins. In a large stainless-steel or coated-aluminum wok or saucepan, combine the water, honey, and star anise. Bring to a boil, reduce the heat, and simmer for 10 minutes, until the honey has dissolved and the liquid is aromatic. Dunk the poussins briefly in the liquid, then remove and pat dry, inside and out. Rub the insides of the poussins with the salt.

In a small bowl, combine the dark soy and five-spice powder. With a pastry brush, paint the mixture all over the birds. Place them on a rack and air-dry for 4 hours (refrigerated if you prefer), or place them in front of a fan and dry for 2 hours. The skin of the birds should feel like parchment.

In a carbon-steel wok, heat the oil over medium-high heat until it is just beginning to smoke. Gently slide the poussins into the oil and deep-fry, turning once, until the skin is crisp and golden brown, and the juices run clear when you prick the birds at the thickest part of the thigh. Carefully remove them to paper towels and drain. When the birds are cool enough to handle, cut them into serving pieces and arrange on a bed of greens to serve.

Crispy Pork with Spicy Thai Flavors

You could toss these crisp pork cubes in any sauce, but here I use spicy fresh Thai flavors. This dish is quite hot, so if you want to, you can reduce the number of chilies or leave them whole. I have used pork butt, as a little fat is great for the flavor. However, you could substitute tenderloin if you don't mind the extra expense and wish to save on the calories.

SERVES 4

$1\frac{1}{2}$ **pounds pork butt**

1 egg, beaten

1 tablespoon cornstarch

$1\frac{1}{2}$ **teaspoons salt**

1 teaspoon freshly ground black pepper

2 cups vegetable oil

4 garlic cloves, minced

6 cilantro plants, including roots, well washed and coarsely chopped

6 dried chilies, crumbled

3 tablespoons fish sauce *(nuoc mam* or *nam pla)*

3 tablespoons fresh lime juice

2 tablespoons water

$\frac{1}{4}$ **cup roasted peanuts, coarsely chopped**

Trim the pork of excess fat and cut into 1 1/2-inch cubes. In a bowl, combine the egg, cornstarch, salt, and black pepper. Add the pork cubes and toss to mix.

In a carbon-steel wok, heat the oil over medium-high heat until just smoking. Add the pork, in batches, and deep-fry until golden brown. Remove to paper towels to drain. When all the pork is cooked, pour off all but 1 tablespoon of the oil; reserve the excess oil for another use or discard.

Return the wok to the heat. Add the garlic, cilantro, and chilies, and stir-fry for 10 seconds. Add the fish sauce, lime juice, and water. Bring to a simmer and cook for 1 minute. Add the pork and peanuts, and toss to coat well with the sauce. Serve immediately.

Real Orange Beef

Deservedly popular on restaurant menus everywhere for its combination of rich meaty flavor and a mellow citrus edge, orange beef, when authentically cooked, should be deep-fried first to give the meat its characteristic chewy texture. Here is a recipe for the real thing.

SERVES 4

1 pound beef filet mignon tails or flank steak
2 tablespoons dark soy sauce
1 tablespoon cornstarch
1 teaspoon freshly ground black pepper
2 cups vegetable oil

For the Sauce

2 pieces dried tangerine peel (about 2 inches long) soaked in warm water and slivered, and ¼ cup of the soaking water reserved
4 slices peeled fresh ginger (each about the size of a quarter), slivered
1 tablespoon slivered orange zest
2 tablespoons dry sherry
½ cup orange juice
2 teaspoons thin soy sauce
1 tablespoon hoisin sauce

1 tablespoon Asian sesame oil

Slice the meat into thin strips about 2 inches long and ¼ inch thick. In a small bowl, combine the dark soy sauce, cornstarch, and pepper. Add the beef, toss to coat well, and let stand for 10 minutes.

In a carbon-steel wok, heat the vegetable oil over medium-high heat until just smoking. Deep-fry the beef slices, in batches, for about 5 minutes, until crisp. Remove to paper towels to drain. Pour off the oil from the wok, and reserve for another use or discard. Do not clean the wok.

Prepare the sauce: Set the wok over a high flame and add the tangerine peel, ginger, and orange zest. Stir-fry for about 30 seconds, until aromatic. Add the sherry, orange juice, thin soy sauce, hoisin sauce, and reserved tangerine water. Bring to a simmer and cook for about 2 minutes, until slightly reduced.

Add the beef to the sauce, and toss to mix and coat well. Drizzle with the sesame oil and serve immediately.

fish and seafood

Shrimp in Their Shells with Black Beans

You must use shrimp with their shells for this recipe. In Chinatown, you will be able to get large shrimp or prawns with their heads on as well. They are perfect for this dish, and if you wish to eat as the Asians do, eat the whole shrimp—head, shell, and all. To me, this is what makes the dish a truly scrumptious feast.

SERVES 4

1 pound large shrimp, preferably with heads, unpeeled
2 cups vegetable oil

For the Sauce
¼ cup fermented black beans
4 garlic cloves, minced
1 tablespoon minced peeled fresh ginger
4 scallions (green and white parts), minced
1 tablespoon thin soy sauce
½ cup Basic Chicken Broth (page 22) or water
1 teaspoon freshly ground black pepper
Salt to taste
2 teaspoons cornstarch mixed with 3 tablespoons cold water

Rinse the shrimp and pat dry with paper towels.

In a carbon-steel wok, heat the oil over high heat until just smoking. Deep-fry the shrimp, in batches, for 5 to 7 minutes, until they just turn pink and the shells are crispy. Remove them to paper towels and drain. Pour off the oil from the wok and reserve for another use or discard. Do not clean the wok.

Prepare the sauce: Rinse the black beans and mash lightly with a fork. Return the wok to high heat. Add the garlic, ginger, scallions, and black beans. Stir-fry for about 30 seconds, until aromatic. Add the soy, broth, and black pepper. Toss to mix well. Season with salt. Add the cornstarch mixture and cook for 1 minute, or until thickened.

Add the shrimp to the sauce and toss to coat well. Serve immediately.

Deep-Fried Whole Fish

Deep-frying whole fish in a conventional pan can be a logistical problem, but when you use a wok, it is effortlessly done. This crispy fish can be topped with any sauce, but I like a sour sauce made with Chekiang black vinegar for its unique mellow flavor.

SERVES 6

1 firm-fleshed whole fish (about 3 to 4 pounds), scaled and
    cleaned
½ cup all-purpose flour
½ cup cornstarch
1 teaspoon salt
½ teaspoon freshly ground black pepper

For the Sauce
1 cup Basic Chicken Broth (page 22)
¼ cup dry white wine
1 tablespoon thin soy sauce
2 tablespoons black vinegar
1 teaspoon sugar
1 tablespoon cornstarch mixed with 2 tablespoons cold water
1 tablespoon Asian sesame oil

2 cups vegetable oil
2 scallions (green and white parts), slivered
2 tablespoons slivered peeled fresh ginger

Rinse the fish in cold water and pat dry with paper towels, inside and out. Combine the flour, cornstarch, salt, and pepper. Dredge the fish in the flour mixture, coating well.

Prepare the sauce: In a small stainless-steel or coated-aluminum wok or saucepan, combine the broth, wine, soy sauce, black vinegar, sugar, cornstarch mixture, and sesame oil. Bring to a simmer and cook for about 5 minutes, until thickened. Keep warm.

In a carbon-steel wok, heat the vegetable oil over high heat until just smoking. Gently slide the fish into the oil and deep-fry for 8 to 10 minutes, until golden. Using a ladle, spoon some of the hot oil over the parts of the fish that are not submerged. Turn the fish once, with two spatulas. When the fish is golden and feels firm when pressed, it is done; the total cooking time should be 20 to 25 minutes, depending on the thickness of the fish. Remove the fish to a serving platter and sprinkle with the scallions and ginger. Reheat 2 tablespoons of the oil to smoking and drizzle over the scallions and ginger, which should sizzle. (The rest of the oil can be discarded, or strained and reused.) Pour the warm sauce over the fish and serve.

Chilean Sea Bass Slices in Wine Sauce

Chilean sea bass is perfect for this dish, as it cuts easily into thin slices, but you can use any firm-fleshed white fish. The spicy sauce is a flavor opposite to that of the delicate fish, creating the yin-yang contrast popular in Chinese cooking.

SERVES 2 TO 4

½ **pound Chilean sea bass**
1 **egg white**
1 **tablespoon cornstarch**
1 **teaspoon thin soy**
2 **cups vegetable oil**

For the Sauce

1 **tablespoon minced peeled fresh ginger**
2 **scallions (green and white parts), minced**
1 **tablespoon yellow bean sauce**
2 **teaspoons chili paste**
¼ **cup dry white wine**
¼ **cup Fish and Shrimp Broth (page 24) or Basic Chicken Broth
    (page 22)**
1 **teaspoon thin soy sauce**
1 **teaspoon freshly ground black pepper**
1 **teaspoon rice vinegar**
Pinch of sugar
¼ **cup green peas**
1 **tablespoon Asian sesame oil**

Slice the fish into pieces about 1½ inches wide by ¼ inch thick. In a medium bowl, combine the egg white, cornstarch, and thin soy. Add the fish slices and coat well. Let stand for 10 minutes.

In a carbon-steel wok, heat the vegetable oil over medium-high heat until just smoking. Deep-fry the fish slices until golden and crisp. Remove them to paper towels to drain. Pour off the oil from the wok, strain, and reserve for another use or discard. Do not clean the wok.

Prepare the sauce: Return the wok to the heat. Add the ginger and scallions, and stir-fry for 30 seconds, until aromatic. Add the bean sauce, chili paste, white wine, broth, soy sauce, black pepper, vinegar, and sugar. Bring to a simmer. Add the peas and stir in the sesame oil.

Add the fish slices to the sauce and simmer for 1 minute, turning to coat well. Serve hot.

Shrimp Wontons

Traditional shrimp wontons are made with finely chopped shrimp, sometimes with some ground pork mixed in. Use tiger shrimp in the mixture for great flavor, if you can find them. The filling is quick and easy to make. When you deep-fry these wontons and serve them with Homemade Plum Sauce (page 188), they make an easy hors d'oeuvre. I also like to mound them on a plate and pour plum sauce or any sweet and sour sauce over them for an entrée in an Asian-style meal.

MAKES 36 WONTONS

½ **pound medium shrimp, peeled and deveined**
½ **pound ground pork (see Note)**
2 **teaspoons salt**
1 **teaspoon freshly ground black pepper**
1 **teaspoon sugar**
2 **teaspoons cornstarch**
1 **tablespoon Asian sesame oil**
36 **square wonton skins**
2 **cups vegetable oil**

In the bowl of a food processor, combine the shrimp, pork, salt, pepper, sugar, cornstarch, and sesame oil. Pulse until the mixture is smooth.

Lay the wonton skins out on a work surface, one dozen at a time. Place a scant teaspoon of the filling in the center of each wrapper. Fold over to form a triangle, then fold the sides over each other and seal with cold water. Arrange in a single layer on a lightly floured tray. When all the wontons are formed, cover them with a clean cloth and refrigerate until ready to use. *Wontons may be made a day in advance.*

In a carbon-steel wok, heat the vegetable oil over medium-high heat until just smoking. Add the wontons, a few at a time, and deep-fry until they are golden brown. Remove with a slotted spoon or mesh skimmer and drain on paper towels. Serve hot.

> **Note:** If you prefer, you can make the filling with shrimp only; substitute an additional ½ pound of peeled shrimp for the ground pork.

Spicy Shrimp Fritters

These fritters are easy to make and outstanding as cocktail nibblies.

MAKES 6 TO 8 APPETIZER SERVINGS

2 eggs, beaten
5 tablespoons all-purpose flour
2 scallions (green and white parts), minced
2 tablespoons chopped cilantro
3 fresh jalapeños, seeded and minced
¼ cup milk mixed with ¼ cup water
1 teaspoon salt
½ teaspoon freshly ground black pepper
½ pound shrimp, peeled, deveined, and coarsely chopped
2 cups light olive or pure olive oil

In a bowl, combine the eggs, flour, scallions, cilantro, jalapeños, milk mixture, salt, and pepper. Whisk to create a smooth batter, and fold in the shrimp.

In a carbon-steel wok, heat the oil over medium-high heat until just beginning to smoke. Drop the batter by heaping teaspoonful into the oil and deep-fry, turning once or twice, for 3 to 5 minutes, until the fritters are a deep golden brown and float to the top. Remove to paper towels to drain. Serve hot.

Squid Rings

Who doesn't love deep-fried squid? I use only cornstarch to coat the squid, as this gives the crispest crust. You can skip the last step and serve the squid simply with a squeeze of lemon or lime juice, but tossing it with salt and chilies makes this a Cantonese classic.

MAKES 6 APPETIZER SERVINGS

2 pounds squid, cleaned
1 cup cornstarch
2 teaspoons salt
1 teaspoon freshly ground black pepper
2 cups vegetable oil
3 dried hot chilies, crumbled
Lemon or lime wedges, for garnish

Cut off the squid tentacles and set aside. Cut the bodies into rings about ½ inch thick. Rinse and drain well. Combine the cornstarch with 1 teaspoon of the salt and the pepper. Dredge the squid rings in the cornstarch mixture, tossing to coat well. Remove to a strainer and bang it once or twice to remove any excess cornstarch.

In a carbon-steel wok, heat the oil over high heat until just smoking. Add the squid, in batches, and deep-fry until golden brown and crisp. Drain well on paper towels. When all the squid is cooked, pour off and discard the oil, or save it for another use. Clean the wok with paper towels.

Return the wok to high heat and add the remaining teaspoon of salt and the chilies, tossing to mix well. Add the squid rings and toss with the spiced salt to coat. Remove to a plate and serve hot, garnished with lemon or lime wedges.

Deep-Fried *Panko* Oysters

There is nothing like a crunchy, crusted deep-fried oyster, with its soft succulent center. These *panko* oysters do not get soggy on the outside even as they cool. They are great eaten alone, or in a po'boy sandwich East-West style. I find that light olive oil and pure olive oil are good oils for deep-frying—they help food stay really crisp.

SERVES 2 TO 4

½ cup all-purpose flour
1½ cups *panko* crumbs
2 eggs, beaten
1 teaspoon salt
½ teaspoon freshly ground white pepper, or Japanese pepper
    (*sansho*)
2 dozen large oysters, shucked
2 cups light olive oil
Ginger-Mustard Mayonnaise (page 187)

Place the flour and *panko* on separate small plates. In a bowl, combine the eggs with the salt and pepper. Dredge the oysters in the flour, then dip them in the egg mixture. Coat well with the *panko* crumbs just before deep-frying.

In a carbon-steel wok, heat the oil over high heat until just smoking. Add the oysters, in small batches, and deep-fry until crisp and golden. Remove and drain on paper towels. Serve with the mayonnaise on the side.

Mushrooms with Clam and Black Bean Stuffing

Either fresh shiitake or dried black mushrooms would work in this recipe but I find the dried mushrooms more flavorful. *Panko* crumbs, made from wheat starch, are used in place of bread crumbs in Japan. I love to cook with them, as they stay crisp even as the food cools.

MAKES 36 PIECES

36 dried Chinese black or fresh shiitake mushrooms

For the Filling
1 tablespoon fermented black beans
3 garlic cloves, minced
2 teaspoons minced peeled fresh ginger
2 teaspoons vegetable oil
2 teaspoons dark miso
1 tablespoon sake
1 tablespoon cornstarch
2 cups fresh shucked clams, minced
1 teaspoon salt
¼ teaspoon Japanese chili pepper *(nanami togarashi)*

½ cup cornstarch
1 egg beaten with 1 tablespoon cold water
1 cup *panko*
2 cups vegetable oil

If using fresh mushrooms, clean them with a damp paper towel and remove the stems. If using dried, soak them in warm water for 15 minutes, until soft; then drain them, reserving their soaking water, and remove and discard the stems.

Prepare the filling: Rinse the black beans to remove any excess salt. In a small bowl, lightly crush together the black beans, garlic, ginger, and oil; do not mash the beans into a paste, as they will become bitter. In another small bowl, mix together the miso, sake, and cornstarch. Add to the black bean mixture, then add the clams, salt, and Japanese chili pepper. Toss to mix well.

Sprinkle the cornstarch onto a piece of wax paper. Press the inside of each mushroom into the cornstarch to coat the inside. Fill the mushrooms with the clam mixture, mounding slightly. Gently dip each mushroom into the egg mixture, then coat with *panko* crumbs.

In a carbon-steel wok, heat the oil over medium-high heat until just smoking. Gently slide the mushrooms into the oil, filling-side down, a few at a time, and deep-fry until golden, turning once. Remove to paper towels to drain. Serve hot.

8

tea-
smoking

In the early '80s, when Peter Kump put together his cooking school on Ninety-second Street in New York, most of us who taught there were friends. It was great fun, and there was a constant exchange of ideas with guest teachers, many of whom were food-world luminaries. We were in and out of one another's classrooms, prepping or sitting in on classes. I walked in one day to find Chris Kump, Peter's son and a superb chef in his own right, fuming because we had no smoker. Once again, the versatile wok saved the day when I showed Chris that the wok makes an excellent smoker. Within an hour he had smoked enough beef filet to serve eighty guests—all done without any special equipment. ● The ancient Chinese method of tea-smoking in a wok takes full advantage of the wok's unique contours. Because the bottom of the wok is narrow, it needs only a few smoking ingredients, while the wider surface near the top accommodates quite a bit of food. Although tea-smoking is a three-part process that can take days, it does not require much effort. The result is food with no added fat and lots of flavor. Smoking also imparts a unique texture.

Also, unless you are smoking many items one after another, using a wok to smoke will hardly set off any smoke alarms in your kitchen. The purpose of smoking is to impart flavor, not to cook food, so in most cases, the technique is applied to precooked food, which requires only a brief smoking time. The texture of tea-smoked food is different from that of smoked raw food. However, you will find a few recipes here that break this rule, especially when it comes to seafood, which would be overcooked and tough if cooked before smoking. Poaching and deep-frying are the favored methods for precooking food to be smoked, and I offer a variety of flavorings for the marinades and poaching mixtures.

Tea-smoking allows you to control the amount of smoke flavor imparted to the food. The basic smoking ingredients remain essentially the same: sugar to create smoke quickly, flour or raw rice to prevent the tea leaves themselves from burning, and the tea leaves to impart the smokiness to the food. Each of these is spread over the bottom of the wok, in turn, making three layers. I have varied the smoke flavor a little by using different teas, and in some cases, I have added a spice or an herb. You can play with your own combinations to create your own unique smoke brand. It is best to cure the smoked food for at least twenty-four hours, to allow the smoke flavor to permeate the food.

Inexpensive carbon-steel woks are best for smoking because they are able to take a lot of dry heat and conduct heat fairly quickly. Lining your wok with aluminum foil obviates the inconvenience of messy cleanups, and often, when I have lined it well, I don't even have to wash my wok after I have smoked in it. A metal rack that will sit at least 2 inches above the smoking ingredients is required; for a 14-inch wok, you'll need a round stainless-steel rack (like the kind for cooling cakes) at least 8 inches across. And, of course, your wok must have a lid. Once you are comfortable with the recipes and timing, keep the lids on after you turn off the heat, and let the smoke dissipate. Don't worry—the food will not overcook or become too bitter.

Tea-smoked dishes are meant to be eaten at room temperature and can be part of main-dish salads. In the Chinese kitchen, smoked food is usually served as an appetizer course at banquets and formal dinners. The use of large amounts of meat and seafood distinguishes these as opulent dishes, but this simple wok technique makes even inexpensive tofu seem special.

Smoked Squab or Quail

The idea for smoking quail came about while I was working with my friend Brad Ogden and his chef, Steve Simmons, on a fund-raising dinner for the Beard Foundation. The teeny quail need a briefer cooking time than squab, but the difference in their smoking times is negligible.

MAKES 8 APPETIZERS

2 tablespoons dark soy sauce
1 tablespoon minced peeled fresh ginger
1 tablespoon minced scallion (green and white parts)
1 tablespoon Japanese pepper *(sansho)*
4 squab or 8 quail

For the Poaching Liquid

1 cup dark soy sauce
2 whole scallions
2 slices fresh ginger (each about the size of a quarter)
1 cassia bark or cinnamon stick
1 tablespoon whole star anise pods
1 tablespoon sugar
6 cups water

For the Smoking Mixture

½ cup sugar
½ cup flour
½ cup Lapsang souchong tea leaves

Asian sesame oil (optional)

In a small bowl, combine the soy, ginger, scallion, and *sansho*. Rub the mixture all over the squab or quail, inside and out. Wrap them well in plastic and refrigerate overnight.

In a 14-inch carbon-steel wok, combine the poaching ingredients: the soy, scallions, ginger, cassia bark, star anise, sugar, and water. Heat to a simmer. Add the birds and simmer over low heat until tender, for 10 to 12 minutes for squab, and 7 to 8 minutes for quail. Remove the birds to a platter and cool for 10 minutes. Drain the liquid from the wok and save for another use or discard. Clean the wok and wipe dry.

Line the wok and lid with aluminum foil. Scatter the smoking mixture over the bottom of the wok: first the sugar, then the flour, and then the tea leaves. Place a metal rack 2 inches above the mixture and lay the birds on the rack. Heat until wisps of smoke rise, then cover the wok tightly and smoke the birds for 20 minutes. Turn off the heat and let stand for 20 minutes, without uncovering, to allow the smoke to dissipate. When the birds are cool, wrap them well and refrigerate for 24 hours. Rub with sesame oil, if desired, and serve.

Tea-Smoked Chicken

Early in my cooking career, I was asked to be on a radio talk show. I brought this chicken as a sample of my food, and the host enjoyed it so much, I got plenty of time to talk about my classes and catering business. Thanks to her, this dish eventually became so popular, I had to excise it from my repertoire, as I got quite bored with making it. It was a pleasant surprise, indeed, when I made it once again for this book, to find that this dish is as good as ever and still makes a wonderful appetizer. The smoky flavor improves after two or three days in the refrigerator, so it is an ideal plan-ahead party dish. Traditionally, smoked chicken is served as part of a cold platter at formal dinners, but don't hesitate to put it in salads or in sandwiches.

MAKES 10 TO 12 APPETIZERS

2 tablespoons salt
2 tablespoons Szechwan peppercorns
1 3-pound chicken, or 2 whole breasts with skin and bones

For the Poaching Liquid
1 cup dark soy sauce
2 whole scallions
2 slices fresh ginger (each about the size of a quarter)
1 cassia bark or cinnamon stick
1 tablespoon whole star anise pods
1 tablespoon sugar
6 cups water

For the Smoking Mixture
¾ cup sugar
¾ cup raw rice
¾ cup black tea leaves

2 tablespoons Asian sesame oil

In a dry carbon-steel wok, toast the salt and Szechwan peppercorns over medium heat for 5 minutes, or until aromatic, stirring constantly to prevent them from burning. Remove from the heat and cool. Rub the flavored salt all over the chicken, inside and out. Place the chicken in a dish, cover tightly with plastic wrap, and refrigerate overnight.

In a large pot or wok, combine the poaching liquid ingredients: the soy, scallions, ginger, cassia bark, star anise, sugar, and water. There should be enough liquid to cover the chicken when it is submerged; if not, add more water. Cover and bring to a boil, reduce the heat, and simmer for 10 to 15 minutes, until the mixture is aromatic. Carefully slide in the chicken, pushing it down to submerge completely. Return the liquid to a simmer, and poach the chicken over low heat for about 20 minutes, or until its juices run clear when it is pierced at the thickest part of the thigh. Do not overcook the chicken. Remove at once to a dish and cool for 10 minutes.

Line a 14-inch carbon-steel wok and lid with aluminum foil. Scatter the smoking mixture over the bottom of the wok: first the sugar, then the rice, and then the tea leaves. Place a metal rack about 2 inches over the mixture. Arrange the chicken on the rack. Heat the wok over medium heat until the sugar just begins to smoke. Immediately cover tightly and continue to smoke for 25 to 30 minutes. Turn off the heat and let stand for 20 to 30 minutes, without uncovering, to allow the smoke to dissipate. Uncover and cool the chicken completely. The chicken will be a lovely mahogany color.

Wrap the chicken well in plastic wrap and refrigerate for at least 1 day before serving. Rub the chicken all over with the sesame oil, cut into bite-size pieces, and serve.

Smoked Tofu

One of the dishes I prepared for a Chinese New Year banquet at the James Beard Foundation was a mixture of dried mushrooms, tree ears, and smoked tofu. Interestingly, when I tasted the smoked tofu by itself, although properly smoky, it had a bitter taste. When cooked with the vegetables in a savory sauce, however, the smokiness mellowed out and the tofu was delicious. Smoked tofu can be used in braised or stewed dishes as well as in stir-fries. Tofu is delicate so a more subtle blend of black tea and jasmine tea works best for smoking. This recipe is really quick and easy, as nothing needs to be done to the tofu before smoking.

MAKES 1 POUND

For the Smoking Mixture
1/2 **cup sugar**
1/2 **cup flour**
1/4 **cup black tea leaves**
1/4 **cup jasmine tea leaves**

1 **pound firm tofu squares**

Line a carbon-steel wok and lid with aluminum foil.

Scatter the smoking mixture over the bottom of the wok: first the sugar, then the flour, and then the tea leaves. Place a metal rack 2 inches above the mixture and arrange the tofu squares on the rack.

Heat the wok over medium heat until smoke wisps are visible. Cover tightly and smoke the tofu for 20 to 25 minutes. Turn off the heat and let sit without uncovering for 30 minutes to allow the smoke to dissipate. Remove the tofu, let it cool and use as desired.

Smoked tofu may be wrapped well in plastic and stored in the refrigerator for 3 to 5 days.

Smoked Duck

I was once asked to cater a wedding reception at the Dakota, the famous apartment building overlooking Central Park on the Upper West Side of Manhattan that has been home to many celebrities. Naturally, I was excited about working in such an illustrious building for a great client, who must remain unnamed. I drew up a sample menu and, wanting to make it extra special, decided to feature a smoked duck salad. I had never prepared the recipe before but included it anyway, thinking that my client would surely want changes to the proposed menu. To my surprise, she loved the menu just as it was written and I was stuck with the prospect of turning out smoked duck for one hundred guests. I have since cut the prep time to three days from five; it's still a major production, but after tasting the duck, I know you will find the effort worthwhile.

If you are using a whole duck, you can butterfly it by cutting down along the back, removing the backbone, and breaking the breastbone so the duck will lie flat. Poultry shears work very well for this job. You can also cut the duck into two halves for easier handling.

SERVES 6

1 5-pound duck, cut up, or 3 whole duck breasts with skin and
    bones intact
2 teaspoons five-spice powder
Zest of 1 orange
1 tablespoon minced peeled fresh ginger
1 scallion (green and white parts), minced
3 tablespoons sake
3 tablespoons dark soy sauce

For the Poaching Liquid
2 cups dark soy sauce
4 slices fresh ginger (each about the size of a quarter)
2 whole scallions
¼ cup (loosely packed) dried tangerine peel
2 teaspoons five-spice powder
3 cups water

For the Smoking Mixture
¾ cup sugar
¾ cup raw rice
½ cup Lapsang souchong tea leaves
¼ cup orange spice tea leaves (about 10 tea bags)

Remove and discard as much of the fat from the duck as possible.

In a small bowl, combine the five-spice powder, orange zest, ginger, scallion, sake, and soy sauce. Rub the mixture all over the duck, inside and out. Wrap the bird well in plastic and refrigerate overnight.

In a deep wok or saucepan, combine the ingredients for the poaching liquid: the soy sauce, ginger, scallions, tangerine peel, five-spice powder, and water. Cover and bring just to a simmer for about 15 minutes, until aromatic. Add the duck and poach for 30 to 35 minutes, or until it is tender and cooked through. Remove to a dish and cool for about 10 minutes. Pour off the poaching liquid and reserve for another use or discard.

Line a carbon-steel wok and lid with aluminum foil. Scatter the smoking mixture over the bottom of the wok: first the sugar, then the rice, and then the tea leaves. Place a metal rack 2 inches above the mixture. Place the duck on the rack and heat over medium heat. When you see wisps of smoke, cover the wok tightly and smoke the duck for 30 minutes. Turn off the heat and let stand, without uncovering, for 20 to 30 minutes to allow the smoke to dissipate. Remove the duck to a plate and cool completely.

Wrap the duck well in plastic and refrigerate for at least 24 hours before serving.

Tea-Smoked Beef

This beef is delicious in a Thai-style salad, or in any salad for that matter. I prefer beef cooked quite rare, but you can cook it to medium-rare by poaching it a bit longer. In the case of rare beef, I suggest you serve it within two to three days; if you won't be able to use a whole tenderloin in that time, freeze half. This technique also works well with Red-Poached Filet Mignon (page 116), in which case you may skip the marinating step.

SERVES 10 TO 12

1 whole beef tenderloin (about 5 pounds), all visible fat removed
1 tablespoon whole star anise pods
3 tablespoons Szechwan peppercorns
2 tablespoons fennel seeds
2 teaspoons whole cloves
¼ cup dark soy sauce
2 tablespoons cognac
2 tablespoons minced peeled fresh ginger
2 scallions (green and white parts), minced
6 garlic cloves, minced

For the Poaching Liquid
2 cups dark soy sauce
½ cup sherry
2 whole scallions
4 slices peeled fresh ginger (each about the size of a quarter)
4 dried hot red peppers
2 tablespoons whole star anise pods
2 tablespoons Szechwan peppercorns
1 tablespoon black peppercorns
3 cups water

For the Smoking Mixture
¾ cup sugar
¾ cup raw rice
¾ cup Lapsang souchong or black tea leaves

Asian sesame oil (optional)

Fold under the tail end of the tenderloin, and tie to create an even thickness throughout. In a dry skillet, toast the star anise, Szechwan peppercorns, fennel, and cloves over medium heat for 3 to 5 minutes, until aromatic. Transfer to a spice grinder or blender and grind to a fine powder.

In a small bowl, combine the spices with the soy, cognac, ginger, scallions, and garlic. Rub the mixture all over the filet, wrap the meat well in plastic, and let stand overnight in the refrigerator.

In a 14-inch carbon-steel wok or large saucepan, combine all the poaching ingredients: the soy, sherry, scallions, ginger, red peppers, star anise, peppercorns, and water. Bring to a simmer, cover, and cook gently for 10 minutes, until aromatic. Cut the tenderloin in half, so it will fit into the wok; then add the beef to the liquid and poach until the internal temperature reaches 115°F. for rare or 125°F. for medium-rare. Remove from the heat and let cool for 10 minutes. Drain off the poaching liquid. Rinse the wok in hot water and wipe dry.

Line the wok and lid with aluminum foil. Scatter the smoking mixture over the bottom: first the sugar, then the rice, and then the tea leaves. Place a metal rack 2 inches above the smoking mixture and arrange the beef on the rack. Heat over medium heat until smoke wisps rise, then cover tightly and smoke the beef for 25 to 30 minutes. Turn off the heat and let stand for 20 to 30 minutes, without uncovering, to allow the smoke to dissipate. Remove the beef to a platter and let cool completely. Wrap well and refrigerate for 24 hours. Rub the beef with sesame oil, if desired, then cut into thin slices and serve.

Smoked Beef on Crunchy Salad

The dark rich look and smoky flavor of the beef contrasts nicely with the light greens and whites of the vegetables. The light dressing keeps the vegetables fresh-tasting as a balance to the rich beef.

SERVES 4

For the Dressing

4 teaspoons grated fresh ginger
1 tablespoon fish sauce (*nuoc mam* or *nam pla*)
6 tablespoons light olive oil
2 tablespoons fresh lemon juice
¼ teaspoon salt
½ teaspoon freshly ground black pepper

1 cup shredded Napa cabbage
1 cup cucumber sticks (each about ¼ inch thick by 2 inches long)
1 cup jicama sticks (each about ¼ inch thick by 2 inches long)
2 cups shredded endive, crisped in ice water and drained
2 cups Tea-Smoked Beef slices (page 168)

In a small bowl, combine the dressing ingredients: the ginger, fish sauce, olive oil, lemon juice, salt, and pepper. Whisk to make a smooth sauce.

In a large bowl, combine the cabbage, cucumber, jicama, and endive. Drizzle with half the dressing and toss lightly. Mound the vegetables on a serving platter. Toss the beef with the remaining dressing and arrange on top of the vegetables. Serve.

Smoked Pork Tenderloins

One of my favorite German dishes is smoked pork loin, so I wondered how pork would take to tea-smoking. I used pork tenderloins, as they cook quickly and stay moist. Homemade Plum Sauce (page 188) is a perfect accompaniment.

SERVES 4

1 tablespoon dark soy sauce

1 tablespoon mirin

2 tablespoons plum wine

1 tablespoon minced peeled fresh ginger

1 teaspoon five-spice powder

1 teaspoon sugar

2 pork tenderloins (about 1½ pounds total), well trimmed

For the Poaching Liquid

1 cup thin soy sauce

1 tablespoon whole star anise pods

1 piece of orange zest (2 inches by ¾ inch)

1 teaspoon whole cloves

¼ cup jasmine tea leaves

3 cups water

For the Smoking Mixture

¼ cup jasmine tea leaves

¼ cup black tea leaves

½ cup sugar

½ cup raw rice

In a bowl, combine the soy, mirin, plum wine, ginger, five-spice powder, and sugar. Rub the mixture all over the pork, wrap the meat in plastic, and refrigerate overnight.

In a 14-inch carbon-steel wok, combine the poaching liquid ingredients: the soy, star anise, orange zest, cloves, tea leaves, and water. Cover and simmer for 15 to 20 minutes, until aromatic. Strain to remove all the solids, and discard them. Return the liquid to the pan. Bring to a simmer and add the pork. Poach for about 15 minutes, or until the pork is done. Remove from the liquid and cool for 10 minutes. Clean the wok in hot water and wipe dry.

Line the wok and lid with aluminum foil. Mix the jasmine and black tea leaves together. Scatter the smoking mixture over the bottom of the wok: first the sugar, then the rice, and then the combined tea leaves. Place a metal rack 2 inches above the smoking mixture and lay the pork on the rack. Heat over medium heat until smoke wisps rise, cover the wok tightly, and smoke the pork for 20 minutes. Turn off the heat and let stand, without uncovering, for 20 to 30 minutes, to allow the smoke to dissipate. Remove the pork to a platter and cool. Cut the meat into thin slices and serve at room temperature, or wrap and refrigerate overnight and serve cold.

Tea-Smoked Lamb

The spices I've used here are Indian-influenced. They give the lamb a rich, complex flavor and marry well with the soy in the poaching liquid. You can serve this lamb warm with Mint Yogurt Sauce (page 187) or at room temperature (not cold) as part of a salad. Have the butcher cut strips from a boned leg of lamb no thicker than 2 inches across. You don't have to go hunting for exotic teas; Bigelow's orange spice tea bags, which are available in supermarkets, work just fine. Dried Chinese orange or tangerine peel, called *chenpi,* has the best flavor for the poaching liquid.

SERVES 6 TO 8

3 cardamom pods
1 teaspoon coriander seeds
1 teaspoon black peppercorns
½ teaspoon whole cloves
½ teaspoon fenugreek seeds
½ teaspoon cayenne
2 tablespoons salt
3 pounds boned leg of lamb, cut into 6 strips (each about
    2 inches across), trimmed of fat and tied

For the Poaching Liquid
2 cups dark soy sauce
2 pieces dried tangerine peel *(chenpi)* (each about 2 inches long)
1 cinnamon stick
3 whole star anise pods
1 teaspoon fennel seeds
3 cups water

For the Smoking Mixture
¾ cup sugar
¾ cup flour
¾ cup orange spice tea leaves (about 30 tea bags)

In a dry skillet, toast the cardamon, coriander, peppercorns, cloves, and fenugreek over medium heat for 5 minutes, or until aromatic. In a spice grinder or blender, process until finely ground. Add the cayenne and salt, and blend. Rub all over the lamb. Wrap well in plastic and refrigerate overnight.

In a 14-inch carbon-steel wok or deep saucepan, combine the ingredients for the poaching liquid: the soy sauce, tangerine peel, cinnamon, star anise, fennel, and water. Cover and bring to a simmer over medium heat. Simmer for 15 minutes, or until the liquid is aromatic. Add the lamb and gently poach for 15 minutes, until the lamb is done but still pink on the inside. Remove the lamb and let cool for about 10 minutes. Drain. Clean the wok and wipe it dry.

Line the wok and lid with aluminum foil. Scatter the smoking mixture over the bottom: first the sugar, then the flour, and then the tea leaves. Place a metal rack 2 inches above the smoking mixture and arrange the lamb strips on the rack. Heat over medium heat. When you see wisps of smoke, cover the wok tightly and smoke the lamb for 20 minutes. Turn off the heat and let stand 30 minutes, without uncovering, until the smoke dissipates. Transfer the lamb to a platter to cool. Serve immediately, or wrap well and refrigerate for 24 hours, and up to 3 days, before serving.

Smoked Fish

The cooking method for smoking fish differs in that the fish is deep-fried rather than poached. The deep-frying step gives the fish a special texture and makes it a little more "chewy" and satisfying. At banquets and formal dinners, smoked fish is traditionally served as an appetizer at room temperature.

MAKES 9 TO 12 APPETIZERS, OR 4 TO 6 ENTRÉES

1 whole fish such as bass or snapper (about 3 pounds), or
   3 pounds fish steaks, such as tuna, salmon, or bass (each
   about 1½ inches thick)
3 tablespoons dark soy sauce
3 tablespoons dry sherry
1 tablespoon sugar
1 tablespoon finely slivered peeled fresh ginger
1 tablespoon finely slivered scallion (green and white parts)
2 garlic cloves, thinly sliced
3 cups vegetable oil, for deep-frying

For the Smoking Mixture
½ cup sugar
½ cup all-purpose flour
½ cup Earl Grey tea leaves
1 tablespoon fennel seeds

For the Dressing
¼ cup thin soy sauce
2 tablespoons rice vinegar
4 teaspoons sugar
1 tablespoon finely slivered peeled fresh ginger
1 tablespoon finely slivered scallion (green and white parts)

If using a whole fish, make 3 slashes almost to the bone on the top side of the fish. Combine the soy, sherry, and sugar, and rub the mixture all over the fish. Press some of the ginger, scallion, and garlic into the slashes, and scatter the rest over the fish. Cover and let stand for 2 hours at room temperature, or 4 hours refrigerated.

In a carbon-steel wok, heat the oil over medium-high heat until just smoking. Carefully slide the fish into the oil and deep-fry for 1 to 2 minutes, until golden and just done. Remove the fish from the oil with a wire mesh strainer or slotted spoon and drain on paper towels. Cool for 15 minutes.

Line a 14-inch carbon-steel wok and lid with aluminum foil. Scatter the smoking mixture over the bottom of the wok: first the sugar, then the flour, then the tea leaves, and finallly the fennel seeds. Place a metal rack 2 inches above the mixture and lay the fish on the rack. Heat over medium heat until you see wisps of smoke. Cover the wok tightly and smoke the fish for 20 to 25 minutes. Turn off the heat and let stand for 20 to 30 minutes, without uncovering, to allow the smoke to dissipate.

While the fish is cooling, mix the dressing ingredients in a small bowl: the soy sauce, vinegar, sugar, ginger, and scallion. Pour the dressing over the fish and serve at room temperature.

Smoked Tamarind Squid

I was once caught out with nothing to serve with drinks just as guests were arriving. I had some squid on hand, and I prepared this recipe at the last minute. Because squid cooks quickly, it is flavored, then smoked raw. Simply cut it into rings to serve.

MAKES 8 APPETIZERS

1 pound whole squid
1 1-inch square tamarind pulp
1 tablespoon dark soy sauce
1 tablespoon plum wine
1 tablespoon (packed) brown sugar
2 teaspoons minced peeled fresh ginger
1 tablespoon vegetable oil

For the Smoking Mixture
½ cup sugar
½ cup flour
½ cup jasmine tea leaves

Clean the squid, removing the hard beak. Soak the tamarind in 2 tablespoons of boiling water and mash into a pulp. In a bowl, combine the tamarind pulp, soy, plum wine, sugar, ginger, and oil. Add the squid and toss to coat well. Cover and refrigerate for 2 or more hours.

Line a 14-inch carbon-steel wok and lid with aluminum foil. Scatter the smoking mixture over the bottom of the wok: first the sugar, then the flour, and then the tea leaves. Place a metal rack 2 inches above the mixture and arrange the squid on the rack. Heat over medium heat until smoke wisps rise. Cover the wok tightly and smoke the squid for 10 to 15 minutes, depending on the size of the squid. Turn off the heat and let stand, without uncovering, for 20 to 30 minutes, to allow the smoke to dissipate. Remove the squid and slice into rings. Serve warm.

Smoked Shellfish

In Asian groceries in Chinatown, you will find baskets of dried scallops and oysters of varying grades, the most costly being as high as $65 per pound. These have a strong smoky flavor that is for some an acquired taste. This recipe produces home-smoked shellfish that is more subtle and delicate, and it works with scallops, shrimp, clams, mussels, or oysters. Except for the scallops, which are commonly sold out of their shells, the shellfish should be left in their shells and given a good scrub and rinse. Because they cook in a very short time, I have deviated from the traditional method by smoking them raw. The smoked shellfish may be marinated in Five-Fragrant-Spice Oil (page 180) or its variation, Clove Oil.

MAKES 6 APPETIZERS

1 tablespoon white miso
1 tablespoon mirin
1 tablepoon sake
2 teaspoons Japanese pepper *(sansho)*
1 pound scrubbed and rinsed shellfish, such as oysters, clams,
    mussels, shrimp, and scallops

For the Smoking Mixture
½ cup sugar
½ cup flour
½ cup black tea leaves
1 tablespoon Szechwan peppercorns

In a bowl, combine the miso, mirin, sake, and Japanese pepper. Add the shellfish and toss to coat well. Cover and refrigerate for 2 to 4 hours.

Line a carbon-steel wok and lid with aluminum foil. Scatter the smoking mixture over the bottom of the wok: first the sugar, then the flour, then the tea leaves and Szechwan peppercorns. Place a metal rack 2 inches above the smoking mixture and place the shellfish on the rack. Over medium heat, heat the wok until smoke wisps rise. Cover the wok tightly and smoke the shellfish for 15 minutes. Turn off the heat and let stand, without uncovering, for 20 to 30 minutes, to allow the smoke to dissipate. Remove the shellfish (discard any that have not opened) and serve, or wrap and refrigerate for 1 day to allow the smoky flavor to develop.

9 favorite condiments, chutneys, and pickles

The dishes in this chapter are not based on cooking in the wok; however, they are seasonings, sauces, and sundry foods that add just the right accent to the many wok-based recipes in this book. A few of them are included simply because they are delicious and easy, and one or two are even unexpectedly cooked in the wok. ● People often hesitate to ask me for a recipe, assuming that we food professionals might be somewhat possessive about our secrets. On the contrary, I am always flattered by their interest and pleased to share my enjoyment of food; in fact, this is what inspired me to write this chapter—I wanted to share my favorite recipes for all the special things I like. These are my shortcuts for adding extra zest to quick meals and giving a mark of distinction to more elaborate or important presentations. ● Flavored salts and oils are easy ways to put a personal stamp on the dishes that you serve. Chefs rely on these flavorings to finish many dishes, and when you try these recipes, you will see just how easy it is for you to do the same. Here you will also find a variety of sauces to complement your wok meals. There are dips to use with steamed foods like dumplings and spring rolls, and a selection of salad dressings. I like to serve a simple salad almost daily, particularly in the summer, and having different dressings to choose from keeps my salads interesting and appetizing. These sauces have all become favorites with my friends and family through the years.

Chutneys and pickles are great finishing touches that don't take much effort to have on hand. Because rice is the basis of most meals in Asia, it is the custom to serve one or more pickles as small side dishes that go well with rice. My homemade pickles are quick to make, and keep for months in the refrigerator; the Fresh Pineapple Pickle (page 198) and the Cucumber Pickles with Shiso (page 197) go especially well with curries. Both the Curried Apple Chutney (page 192) and the Mango Chutney (page 193) make wonderful gifts—if you spend a little time preparing a double or triple batch, you can always have on hand a special homemade house gift or holiday present. When canned properly, they will keep on the shelf a very long time.

Though these recipes do not necessarily involve the use of a wok (or any cooking pot at all), I have used a wok to make all the chutneys. Experience has taught me that when you are cooking a large batch of fruit, it is easier to mix and turn the chutney in a wok, and if carefully handled, the fruit will not become too mushy. Because the chutneys can be acidic, a stainless-steel wok is the ideal one to use, but a well-tempered carbon-steel wok works as well, as long as you do not let the chutney stand too long after it is done.

Here, too, you will find recipes for homemade curry pastes. For people who use a wok as a matter of course, having ready-made pastes that require a large number of ingredients makes it easy to toss a spoonful or two into the wok for the necessary quick stir-frying step that cooks the raw taste out of curry. Although the list of ingredients for the curry pastes may seem a little intimidating, once you have a batch made up it keeps well in the refrigerator, and there is no substitute for the taste. I often prepare a batch when I have the ingredients at hand, particularly when I want to use up extra chilies or cilantro, and so I always have the pastes ready to use for quick preparation of different curries.

Garlic Spice Salt

My friend Brad Ogden makes a signature herbal garlic salt that he uses on everything at his restaurant, the Lark Creek Inn, in California. This recipe is the best way to flavor salt with garlic that I know of. I've substituted Asian spices for the fresh herbs of the original blend, and the result is an addictive seasoning to sprinkle on fish, steaks, or chicken. I like this salt so much that I use it to flavor everything, including salads, eggs, and even popcorn.

MAKES 1 CUP

1 head of garlic
1 cup kosher salt
2 teaspoons cumin seeds
1 teaspoon coriander seeds
4 cardamom pods
1 teaspoon black peppercorns
1 teaspoon white peppercorns
$\frac{1}{2}$ teaspoon ground allspice
6 whole cloves
$\frac{1}{2}$ teaspoon freshly grated nutmeg

Peel the garlic and combine with the salt in a mortar or deep bowl. With a pestle or the back of a heavy spoon, crush the garlic cloves into the salt until the salt is damp and smells of garlic. Strain the salt through a coarse sieve to remove the garlic pulp.

In a small carbon-steel wok over low heat, toast the cumin, coriander, cardamom, black and white peppercorns, allspice, and cloves. Cool, and grind in a spice grinder or blender. Add the nutmeg and then the spice mixture to the garlic salt, tossing to mix well. Transfer to a glass jar, and store, covered, in the refrigerator; the salt will keep for several weeks.

Anise Pepper Salt

This licorice-flavored salt may be used as a dip for crispy deep-fried foods or as a flavoring in cooking. It is a variation of the traditional Chinese wild-pepper salt served with crispy squab or chicken.

MAKES ABOUT 1 CUP

1 tablespoon star anise pods
2 teaspoons fennel seeds
½ teaspoon whole cloves
2 teaspoons Szechwan peppercorns
1 tablespoon black peppercorns
½ cup kosher salt

In a dry carbon-steel wok, toast the star anise, fennel seeds, cloves, Szechwan peppercorns, and black peppercorns over low heat until aromatic. Cool, and grind in a spice grinder. Transfer to an 8-ounce glass jar and shake to combine. This flavored salt can be stored, tightly covered, for several weeks.

Five-Fragrant-Spice Oil

This oil would go well with foods that have a natural sweetness to them; it can be used to flavor root vegetables, such as carrots, parsnips, turnips, pumpkins, and winter squashes, and to cook "sweet" meats, such as pork. It also works well in braises that have complex flavorings.

MAKES ½ CUP

½ cup safflower or any other neutral oil
1 teaspoon five-spice powder
Pinch of salt

In a small wok or saucepan, warm the oil with the five-spice powder and salt over low heat. Do not let the oil smoke. Let stand until cool, then transfer to a glass jar or bottle. When completely cold, cover and let stand at room temperature for 24 hours before using. Store at room temperature for a few days or refrigerate for longer storage.

Variation: Clove Oil. Substitute 2 tablespoons of ground cloves for the five-spice powder and eliminate the salt; prepare as above.

Turmeric Oil

This is a wonderful oil to drizzle over cooked vegetables instead of butter. It is particularly good with green beans.

MAKES 1 CUP

1 cup vegetable or light olive oil
1 tablespoon ground turmeric
2 garlic cloves, crushed
1 teaspoon salt

Heat 1 tablespoon of the oil in a small carbon-steel wok or saucepan over low heat. Stir-fry the ground turmeric for about 20 seconds, or until aromatic. Add the remaining oil and the garlic cloves. Heat until the oil just begins to smoke. Remove from the heat and stir in the salt. Cool the oil completely, then pour into a glass jar and let stand for several hours or overnight. Remove the garlic and discard. Cover tightly and refrigerate the oil; it keeps for months.

Black Sesame, Scallion, and Garlic Oil

I recently found black sesame seed oil in Chinatown. This oil is a little darker than regular sesame oil, and is believed to contain tonic qualities that are beneficial to women. Traditionally, scallion oil is used as a dip for white-poached chicken. This slightly different version is a little more pungent.

MAKES 1 CUP

1 teaspoon black sesame seeds
4 scallions (green and white parts), finely minced
2 garlic cloves, minced
¾ cup safflower or canola oil
¼ cup black sesame oil
1 teaspoon salt

In a dry carbon-steel wok, toast the black sesame seeds over medium-low heat for about 10 seconds. Transfer to a plate to cool.

In a large heatproof bowl, combine the scallions and garlic.

In the wok or a saucepan, combine the safflower oil and sesame oil, and add the salt. Heat the mixture over low heat until the oil just begins to smoke, and immediately pour over the scallions and garlic. Cool. Sprinkle with the black sesame seeds just before serving.

Mirin Miso Vinaigrette

Mirin, a sweet Japanese cooking wine, is a wonderfully versatile ingredient. I like to add a bit to any fish marinade to give the fish a nice glaze when it is cooked. Mirin also plays an important role in teriyaki dishes. In this recipe the wine gives the dressing a bit of a kick—balancing the fresh tang of the ginger. If you find this a little sweet for your taste, add a pinch of salt. Use this vinaigrette to dress any salad.

MAKES ABOUT ³/₄ CUP

2 tablespoons white miso
2 tablespoons mirin
1 teaspoon Dijon mustard
1 teaspoon freshly ground black pepper
1 tablespoon fresh lemon juice
2 teaspoons honey
1 tablespoon safflower oil
2 teaspoons grated peeled fresh ginger

In a small bowl, mix together the miso, mirin, mustard, black pepper, and lemon juice. Whisk to blend well. Add the honey and whisk in. Slowly drizzle in the oil while whisking the dressing. Stir in the ginger.

Orange Miso Vinaigrette

I am often asked by students to duplicate the salad dressings they have in Japanese restaurants. This vinaigrette is the result of one of these trials. It goes well with any seafood, in a salad or otherwise.

MAKES ABOUT ¹/₂ CUP

2 teaspoons white miso
1 teaspoon minced peeled fresh ginger
¼ teaspoon freshly ground black pepper
2 tablespoons Basic Vegetable Broth (page 17) or any fish stock
2½ tablespoons fresh orange juice
1 tablespoon canola oil
1 teaspoon Asian sesame oil
1 teaspoon orange zest

In a small bowl, combine the miso, ginger, and pepper. Slowly whisk in the broth to smooth out the miso. Add the orange juice and whisk in the canola and sesame oils in a steady stream to form a creamy dressing. Stir in the orange zest. The dressing can be stored in the refrigerator for up to several weeks.

Hot Red Pepper Vinaigrette

A true East-West blend of hot and tart, this vinaigrette is not only tasty but great looking, especially when used to dress a green vegetable, such as wok-steamed broccoli florets, green beans, or asparagus. It's also a marvelous cold dressing for pasta salads or noodles.

If you can get Spanish pequillo peppers, use them. These come already roasted, in cans or jars, and are available in specialty food stores. They are simply delicious, and although they are rather expensive, you do not have to buy the perfect whole peppers—the pieces will do. Umeboshi plums give the dressing a tart finish.

MAKES 1 1/2 TO 2 CUPS

```
2 umeboshi plums, pitted
2 teaspoons Dijon mustard
1 teaspoon salt
1/2 teaspoon freshly ground black pepper
1/4 cup red wine vinegar
3/4 cup virgin olive oil
1/2 cup diced roasted red peppers (about 3 whole peppers)
1 teaspoon Thai chili paste, or more to taste
```

In a bowl, mash the umeboshi plums into a paste. Add the mustard, salt, black pepper, and vinegar, and whisk together. Slowly drizzle in the oil, whisking constantly until emulsified. Add the red peppers and chili paste. Whisk to blend.

Grated Stem Ginger Dressing

There is nothing quite as fresh tasting as new stem ginger—that is, the waxy young gingerroot with pinkish tinges and no brown skin. This ginger is usually available in the late spring and early fall.

MAKES 1 CUP

1 tablespoon grated fresh stem ginger
1½ teaspoons salt
1 teaspoon freshly ground black pepper
¼ cup rice vinegar
¾ cup light olive oil
½ teaspoon sugar

In a small bowl, combine the ginger, salt, pepper, and vinegar. Gradually whisk in the olive oil. Add the sugar and stir to mix. The dressing will be thin; it will keep in the refrigerator for several weeks.

Umeboshi Plum Dressing

Umeboshi plums are very tart pickled Japanese plums that have their own special taste. They are also quite salty. This dressing is great on fruit salads, as its tartness balances the sugar in the fruit. It is also good on a crisp green salad.

MAKES ½ CUP

3 umeboshi plums
2 teaspoons white miso
1 tablespoon plum wine
1 teaspoon Japanese pepper *(sansho)*
2 tablespoons light olive oil
1 tablespoon mirin
2 tablespoons apple juice
1 shiso leaf, coarsely chopped

In a small bowl, mash the umeboshi plums. Add the miso, plum wine, and Japanese pepper. Stir to blend. Whisk in the oil, mirin, and apple juice. Stir in the shiso, and let sit about 10 minutes for the flavors to marry. If the dressing is too tart, add a little more apple juice. If not using immediately, store in the refrigerator; it keeps well.

dips and sauces

Spicy Chili Dip

Quick and easy, this dip is perfect for dumplings.

MAKES ½ CUP

¼ cup thin soy sauce
2 teaspoons sambal oelek or chili paste

Mix the soy sauce with the sambal oelek.

Lemon-Chili Soy Dip

There are many ways to jazz up soy sauce as a dip. This one is particularly good with dumplings and spring rolls. You can make the sauce spicier or less so by adjusting the amount of chili. If fresh hot chilies are not available, use 1 teaspoon or more of dried chili flakes.

MAKES ABOUT 1 CUP

1 tablespoon fresh lemon juice
4 small hot fresh chilies, minced
3 tablespoons thin soy sauce
2 tablespoons fish sauce (*nuoc mam* or *nam pla*)
1 teaspoon minced peeled fresh ginger
1 teaspoon sugar
2 tablespoons water

In a small bowl, mix together the lemon juice, minced chilies, soy, fish sauce, ginger, sugar, and water. If not using immediately, transfer to a glass jar and store, covered, in the refrigerator, where it will keep indefinitely.

Variation: For a more Thai-influenced sauce, leave out the soy sauce and use ¼ cup of fish sauce. Substitute lime juice for the lemon juice.

Black Vinegar Dipping Sauce

Dipping sauces made with vinegar and julienned ginger are commonly served with dumplings to balance the richness of the dumpling fillings. Instead of the usual red or white rice vinegar, I have used Chinese black vinegar from Chekiang, which, though mild, has a very distinctive taste. Do not combine the ginger and black vinegar too far in advance, as the vinegar will turn the ginger an unappealing dark color.

MAKES ¼ CUP

¼ cup Chinese black vinegar
1 tablespoon finely shredded peeled fresh ginger

Combine the vinegar and ginger in a small bowl not more than 10 minutes before serving.

Kaffir Lime Butter

Kaffir lime leaves have a strong, perfumed, citruslike flavor. They can be purchased fresh in Asian markets (which is best), but if these are hard to find, use the more readily available frozen leaves. Although they keep awhile in your freezer, the flavor dissipates with time; when the leaves turn black, it is time to throw them out. This delicately flavored butter would be good on plain white-poached fish, chicken, pasta, or mild vegetables.

MAKES 1 CUP

16 Kaffir lime leaves
½ pound (2 sticks) unsalted butter
Salt and freshly ground black pepper to taste

Roll the lime leaves tightly, cigarette-fashion, and slice into fine shreds. In a small saucepan, melt the butter, add the lime leaves, and let steep for a few minutes over very low heat, until the butter is flavored and aromatic. Pour through a strainer into a small bowl; discard the lime leaves. Season the butter with salt and pepper to taste, and serve hot.

Ginger-Mustard Mayonnaise

"Doctoring" mayonnaise to make a variety of sauces is an old catering trick. Here is a tried-and-true sauce I have used often, and with great success. You can make your own mayonnaise for this variation, or you can use a bottled one.

MAKES 1 CUP

1 cup mayonnaise
1 teaspoon minced peeled fresh ginger
1 tablespoon Dijon mustard
1 teaspoon wasabi powder
2 teaspoons fresh lemon juice

In a bowl, whisk together the mayonnaise, ginger, mustard, wasabi, and lemon juice. Let stand for at least 10 minutes before using.

Mint Yogurt Sauce

This quick, easy sauce is wonderful with any spicy meat, poultry, or fish. It is especially nice served on the side with curries or even as a dip for crudités.

MAKES 1 CUP

1 cup plain fat-free yogurt
¾ teaspoon salt
2 tablespoons fresh mint leaves, finely shredded
1 tablespoon fresh lemon juice

In a small bowl, combine the yogurt, salt, mint leaves, and lemon juice. Let stand for 10 to 15 minutes for the flavors to develop. Store any leftover sauce in the refrigerator for up to 1 week.

Homemade Plum Sauce

Once you've tried this plum sauce, you'll never go for the bottled stuff again. It is really easy to prepare, and if you use red plums, the sauce will be a beautiful bright red, a color that signifies good fortune to the Chinese. Try this with roast meats, particularly cold roast beef or pork. I like a good dollop in a barbecue sauce or marinade, but be careful—this sauce *is* spicy!

MAKES ABOUT 3 CUPS

4 medium red, yellow, or green plums (about 1 pound)
4 slices peeled fresh ginger (each about the size of a quarter)
1 small red onion, thinly sliced
¼ cup candied ginger, sliced
3 red chilies, dried or fresh
½ cup cider vinegar
¼ cup sugar
2 teaspoons salt

Wash the plums, cut them in half, and remove the pits. Slice the plums into ½-inch pieces.

Place the plums, fresh ginger, onion, candied ginger, chilies, vinegar, sugar, and salt in a small wok. Bring to a boil, reduce the heat, and simmer for about 15 minutes, or until the plums break up and the sauce thickens slightly. Remove from the heat and cool completely. Store in a glass jar and refrigerate, covered; the sauce will keep for several months.

curry pastes

Sri Lankan Curry Paste

When I lived in London, I learned all about Sri Lanka and Sri Lankan curries from my friend Ann McEwan, a tea planter's daughter who grew up in Ceylon. We used to go to a little place on Kensington High Street for our favorite Sri Lankan fish curry at least once a month. Curries from Sri Lanka are made with roasted spices, so the curries are darker. They are also usually very hot and spicy. Use this curry blend with fish, such as cod or even salmon, preferably cut in steaks (a cut that does not seem to be very popular these days) because that way more of the flavor penetrates the fish. If you like, you can cook the dry ingredients well ahead of time; you will have a dry powder that can be stored on the shelf. Add the garlic just before you use the curry paste.

MAKES ³/₄ CUP

5 green cardamom pods
10 dried curry leaves
2 teaspoons cayenne
1 cinnamon stick
½ cup coriander seeds
¼ cup cumin seeds
2 tablespoons fennel seeds
1 teaspoon fenugreek seeds
4 large garlic cloves, minced

In a blender or spice grinder, combine the cardamom, curry leaves, cayenne, and cinnamon. Grind to a coarse powder.

In a dry carbon-steel wok, toast the coriander, cumin, fennel, and fenugreek seeds, stirring frequently so they do not burn. Add the ground cardamom, curry leaves, cayenne, and cinnamon, and toast another 20 to 30 seconds. Cool and transfer to a blender or spice grinder. Grind the spices until you have a fine powder. Add the garlic and grind the mixture into a paste. Remove to a glass jar. Store, covered, in the refrigerator, where it will keep for up to 1 month.

Green Curry Paste

You can make a big batch of this curry paste and store it in the refrigerator in a covered jar. It makes good coconut-based curry and can also be used in soups. Be sure to fry the curry paste a little before adding liquid to your dish; this will cook off the raw taste. The cilantro and green chilies give it its bright color and also a nice freshness.

MAKES 2 CUPS

2 stalks lemongrass
5 green chilies, such as serranos or jalapeños, seeded
1 medium onion, quartered
7 garlic cloves, peeled
2 to 3 cilantro plants with roots
1½-inch piece of frozen galangal, or fresh if available
1 tablespoon vegetable oil
2 teaspoons shrimp paste
1 teaspoon turmeric
1½ teaspoons ground coriander
1 teaspoon ground cumin
1½ teaspoons salt
1 teaspoon freshly ground black pepper

Remove the coarse outer leaves from the lemongrass. Cut off and discard the green parts. Slice the white part of the stalks very thinly. In a food processor, combine the chilies, onion, garlic, cilantro, and galangal. Pulse to chop finely. Remove to a bowl and stir in the lemongrass.

In a carbon-steel wok, heat the oil over medium heat. Add the shrimp paste and stir-fry for about 1 minute, or until aromatic. Add the turmeric, coriander, and cumin. Continue to stir-fry for another 30 seconds to 1 minute. Remove from the heat. Cool. Scrape the stir-fried spices into the bowl with the cilantro mixture. Add salt and pepper to taste. Mix well.

Red Curry Paste

My favorite Thai-style curry paste is great for many things, including beef, pork, lamb, and chicken, and can be used to flavor almost any dish in which you want a bit of spice. It keeps well in a tightly covered glass jar in the refrigerator, so if you like it, make a double batch.

MAKES ABOUT 1 CUP

8 dried red chilies (each about 2 inches long)
1½ tablespoons coriander seeds
2 teaspoons cumin seeds
1 tablespoon black peppercorns
1 tablespoon minced fresh or frozen galangal, or peeled fresh
  ginger
6 garlic cloves
1 piece of lime zest (about 2 inches long and ½ inch wide)
6 cilantro plants with roots, very well washed
2 teaspoons shrimp paste
1 tablespoon salt
2 stalks lemongrass

Pinch the ends off the chilies and remove the seeds. In a dry carbon-steel wok or skillet, toast the coriander and cumin seeds over low heat until aromatic. Combine the chilies, coriander, cumin, and peppercorns in a spice grinder or blender, and grind to a powder.

In a food processor, combine the galangal, garlic, lime zest, cilantro, shrimp paste, and salt. Pulse until chopped. Add the dry spices and continue to pulse until you have a paste.

Remove the coarse outer leaves from the lemongrass and discard the green tops. Slice the white parts very finely and stir into the curry paste.

chutneys and pickles

Curried Apple Chutney

I made this chutney for the first time when my daughter, Samantha, went apple picking with her kindergarten class. Needless to say, those apples were far from perfect, but the chutney turned out great just the same. All the friends and relatives who got a jar that Christmas agreed!

Although any apples will work, I have specified the ever readily available Golden Delicious here. I find that cooking this chutney in a wide wok allows me to blend the ingredients without crushing the apples, and they cook more evenly and do not become mushy.

MAKES 4 CUPS

4 pounds Golden Delicious apples
3 tablespoons vegetable oil
1 ounce fresh ginger, peeled and sliced
2 heads of garlic, cloves peeled and sliced
8 to 10 jalapeños, seeded and thinly sliced crosswise
2 teaspoons fennel seeds
1 teaspoon black peppercorns
2 teaspoons ground turmeric
1 tablespoon ground cumin
1 tablespoon cayenne
1 cup sugar
¾ cup white vinegar

Peel and core the apples, then cut them into slices about 1 inch wide.

In a stainless-steel or coated-aluminum wok, heat the oil over low heat. Add the ginger and garlic, and stir-fry for 1 or 2 minutes. Add the jalapeños, fennel seeds, peppercorns, turmeric, cumin, and cayenne, and stir-fry for another minute, stirring to blend. Add the apples, sugar, and vinegar, toss, and simmer for 10 to 15 minutes, until the apples are tender, stirring once or twice. The apples should not be mushy. Cool and transfer to sanitized glass jars. Cover and refrigerate. The chutney will keep for months.

Mango Chutney

Left, after a catering job, with half a case of mangoes that were getting riper by the minute, I decided to make a tropical-inspired chutney. This delicious condiment is as tasty with roast lamb as with traditional curries and even cold roast beef. If you don't enjoy canning, don't bother; this chutney won't be around long and it will keep in the refrigerator for several months.

MAKES 2 QUARTS

8 ripe mangoes (about 4 pounds)
7 to 10 juicy limes
2 tablespoons vegetable oil
6 to 8 garlic cloves, crushed
4 teaspoons minced peeled fresh ginger
1 teaspoon ground turmeric
1 tablespoon mustard seed
2 teaspoons coriander seeds
2 teaspoons cumin seeds
2 teaspoons cardamom pods
1 teaspoon fennel seeds
8 to 10 small red chilies, fresh or dried, left whole
2 to 4 bay leaves
2 tablespoons salt
2 teaspoons freshly ground black pepper
¼ to ½ cup sugar, depending on sweetness of the mangoes

Cut the mangoes lengthwise as close to the pit as possible. Score the flesh side in large cubes, turn the halves inside out, and cut off the skin. Cut off any flesh left on each side of the pit, remove the skin, and cut the flesh into cubes. Juice enough of the limes to give you 1 cup of juice. Wash the remaining limes and slice thinly.

In a large stainless-steel or coated-aluminum wok deep enough to hold all the fruit, heat the oil over medium heat. Stir-fry the garlic and ginger briefly, for about 30 seconds. Add the turmeric, mustard seeds, coriander seeds, cumin seeds, cardamom, and fennel seeds. Stir-fry for another 30 seconds, add the mango cubes, lime juice, chilies, bay leaves, salt, pepper, and sugar. Bring to a simmer and cook for about 8 minutes, or until the mangoes are tender but hold their shape. Gently turn once or twice. Do not overcook, as the mangoes will turn to mush. Remove the bay leaves and discard. Cool and pour into sterile jars or other covered containers. Cover the containers with their lids, and place them in a water bath. When the water returns to the boil, process for 25 minutes to sterilize. Or, if you prefer, store the jars in the refrigerator.

Two-Eggplant Relish

The little green Thai pea eggplants add an interesting crunch to this relish, though small regular eggplants work, too. Galangal, or *laos*, which is a rhizome of the ginger family, can be purchased frozen or dried in Asian markets. I prefer frozen galangal, as it has more flavor than the dried. Before using dried galangal, soak it in warm water for 10 minutes.

MAKES ABOUT 3½ CUPS

1 pound Asian eggplant or young regular eggplant
½ pound Thai pea eggplants
Salt, for salting eggplant pieces, plus 1 tablespoon
1 piece of tamarind pulp (about the size of a walnut)
1 cup warm water
1 teaspoon shrimp paste
1 teaspoon ground turmeric
1 tablespoon vegetable oil
1 tablespoon minced shallot
1 tablespoon minced peeled fresh ginger
2 garlic cloves, minced
1 1-inch piece of galangal, crushed
4 to 6 small red chilies, or 2 jalapeños, sliced
2 Kaffir lime leaves
1 tablespoon fish sauce (*nuoc mam* or *nam pla*)
¼ cup cider vinegar
2 limes, washed and quartered
1 tablespoon sugar
Juice of 1 lime

Wash and peel the eggplants. Cut the Asian eggplant into large chunks, and place in a colander. Sprinkle liberally with salt and let stand for 30 to 40 minutes in the sink. Rinse well and pat dry with paper towels. Halve the pea eggplants.

In a small bowl, combine the tamarind pulp with the warm water. Mash the pulp with your fingers to break it up.

Place the shrimp paste on a small piece of foil and wrap tightly. Place the foil package directly on the gas flame or on the electric burner and toast for 1 minute, turning once or twice. Remove from the heat and cool.

In a dry skillet, toast the turmeric for 5 seconds over medium heat, stirring to prevent burning.

Heat the oil in a carbon-steel wok over medium heat. Add the shallot, ginger, garlic, and turmeric, and stir-fry for 30 seconds, or until aromatic. Add all the eggplant pieces, toss once or twice, then add the galangal, chilies, lime leaves, fish sauce, vinegar, limes, 1 tablespoon of salt, sugar, and tamarind water. Scrape the shrimp paste into the mixture, and stir to blend well. Bring to a simmer and cook until the eggplant pieces are tender. Stir in the lime juice and cook for another 10 minutes. Remove the lime leaves and discard. Cool and pour into sterile glass jars. Cover and store in the refrigerator, where the relish will keep for several weeks.

Pickled Lotus Root

Simple homemade pickles are a major part of the Asian kitchen. A basic mix of rice vinegar and sugar with a pinch of salt can be used to pickle just about any vegetable. This fresh lotus root pickle is particularly good with rice and is used as an ingredient in sushi. It is also a very pretty edible garnish that has a natural crunch. I like to have a supply of this pickle in my refrigerator and will make some anytime I see fresh lotus root in the market. It keeps almost forever if properly stored.

MAKES ABOUT 1 QUART

1 piece of fresh lotus root (about 8 ounces)
1 cup rice vinegar
1 cup water
1 to 2 tablespoons sugar
1 or 2 shiso leaves, cut in this strips
Pinch of salt

Peel the lotus root and slice very thinly. Place in a bowl of acidulated water to prevent discoloration.

Combine the vinegar, water, sugar, shiso leaves, and salt in a saucepan. Bring to a simmer over low heat and cook until the sugar is dissolved. Drain the lotus slices and place in a sterile jar large enough to hold all the vinegar mixture. Pour the hot liquid over the lotus root. Cool slightly, seal tightly, and refrigerate for at least several days before using. Store refrigerated.

Fresh Cabbage Pickle

This pickle keeps very well in the refrigerator. The turmeric gives it a pretty, delicate color as well as flavor. If you like your food hot and spicy, add more cayenne and hot chilies. You can use fresh or dried chilies for this recipe.

MAKES 1 QUART

1 pound Chinese cabbage
1 tablespoon Szechwan peppercorns
2 teaspoons black mustard seeds
½ teaspoon coriander seeds
¼ teaspoon ground turmeric
2 cups white vinegar
¼ cup sugar
1 teaspoon salt
2 slices fresh peeled ginger (each about the size of a quarter)
¼ teaspoon cayenne
2 jalapeños, seeded and thinly sliced
2 garlic cloves, crushed

Wash the cabbage and cut into 1-inch-wide strips. You will have about 8 cups, lightly packed. In a small skillet, dry-roast the Szechwan peppercorns, mustard seeds, coriander seeds, and turmeric for about 30 seconds, or until aromatic.

In a stainless-steel wok that is large enough to hold all the cabbage, combine the roasted spices with the vinegar, sugar, salt, and ginger, and bring the vinegar mixture to a boil over medium heat. Reduce the heat to low and simmer the mixture until the sugar dissolves. Add the cabbage and cook, turning often, for about 1 minute, just until the cabbage wilts. Remove from the heat and stir in the cayenne, jalapeños, and garlic. Cool and transfer to a clean glass jar. Store in the refrigerator for 1 day before serving. This pickle keeps well in the refrigerator for up to several months.

Cucumber Pickles with Shiso

The long seedless cucumbers commonly called English or European cucumbers are excellent for this recipe; or you can use the tiny Japanese variety that has a sweeter skin. Even regular or Kirby cucumbers may be pickled this way. If they have too many seeds, cut them in half lengthwise and seed them with a teaspoon—your pickles will then have half-moon shapes. These pickles remain crisp and crunchy.

MAKES ABOUT 1 QUART

4 small Japanese cucumbers, or 1 long seedless (about ¾ to
   1 pound)
2 teaspoons salt
1 whole shiso leaf, plus 2 leaves cut into thin ribbons
½ cup rice vinegar
½ cup plum wine
2 tablespoons sugar
2 shallots, thinly sliced crosswise
8 white peppercorns

Wash the cucumbers, pat dry, and slice ⅛ inch thick. Layer the cucumber slices in a bowl, sprinkling each layer with salt. Push the whole shiso leaf down into the center of the layers. Let stand for 2 to 3 hours.

Meanwhile, in a small stainless-steel wok, combine the vinegar, plum wine, shiso shreds, sugar, shallots, and peppercorns. Bring to a boil, reduce the heat, and simmer for 10 minutes, until the sugar is completely dissolved and the mixture is fragrant. Remove from the heat and let cool completely.

Drain the cucumbers and pour the pickling mixture over them. Refrigerate overnight before serving. The pickles may be transferred to a covered glass jar and stored in the refrigerator indefinitely.

Fresh Pineapple Pickle

Zubin Mehta, the famous conductor, always carries a little silver box containing his personal supply of hot red chilies when dining out. I served this pickle at a dinner for him, and he admitted he did not need his stash. You can reduce the quantity of cayenne if you like it milder. This pickle is great with curries and rich stews. It is also good served as a nibble before an Asian-style meal. If the pineapple is not sweet, add 1 to 2 tablespoons of sugar.

MAKES 4 CUPS

1 ripe fresh pineapple
¼ cup white vinegar
1 tablespoon cumin seeds, toasted
1½ teaspoons cayenne, or to taste
½ teaspoon salt

Peel and core the pineapple. Cut into chunks about 1 inch square.

In a bowl, toss the pineapple with the vinegar, cumin seeds, cayenne, and salt. Remove to a covered container and refrigerate overnight before serving. This pickle will keep for months in the refrigerator.

10

sweets

Here are just a few desserts to show that the wok's versatility doesn't end with the main course. I have based all the recipes in this chapter on cooking methods that are used elsewhere in this book, and of course, they can all be prepared in the wok. ● You may not be familiar with many Asian desserts because they do not play a prominent role in most Asian cuisines. As a rule, Asians like cool fresh fruit or hot sweet soups at the end of their meals. Cakes, cookies, puddings—what Westerners think of as dessert—are generally reserved for special festivals. And many Asian sweets do not appeal to the Western palate, as they often mix sweet and salty flavors and contain meat and even bits of fat. Those I've assembled here, while based on traditional ingredients and flavors, are perfectly suited to any cross-cultural meal and will please dinners East *and* West. ● The poached fruit desserts take the Asian preference for fresh fruit one step further, and because fruit cooks more evenly when poached in a single layer, the wok makes the ideal cooking vessel. Steamed Five-Spice Sweet Potato Cake (page 201) is quickly and easily prepared in a bamboo basket and wok, and you will find that cooking it this way gives a nice touch of moistness to the cake. Deep-frying in a wok is a technique much loved in Asia, and it has contributed two excellent desserts—Ginger Puffs (page 204) and Toffee Bananas (page 205). The Jade Sea Pudding (page 203) is a dessert in the sweet soup tradition, but it is thicker and more puddinglike—a very modern Hong Kong–style sweet that is great in summer.

All these recipes are easy and require no special pastry skills, so indulge yourself and enjoy the finale to your Asian-style meals.

Steamed Five-Spice Sweet Potato Cake

Because even today ovens are rare in Asian homes, cakes are steamed in a wok instead of being baked in the oven. They are more moist and a little heavier than a baked cake, but they do taste delicious. This blend of Chinese five spices with sweet potato makes a fall dessert. Steam the cake in a pretty soufflé dish from which it can also be served.

This recipe uses no cream or nuts. The tablespoon of butter is for greasing the pan, and the half cup of oil translates to less than a tablespoon per serving—so this is really a low calorie treat.

SERVES 10

1 pound sweet potatoes
1 tablespoon unsalted butter
All-purpose flour, for dusting
Zest of 1 orange
2 cups all-purpose flour
1 teaspoon baking powder
1 teaspoon baking soda
2 teaspoons Chinese five-spice powder
¼ teaspoon salt
3 large eggs
½ cup vegetable oil
1 cup sugar
½ cup nonfat buttermilk
Confectioners' sugar, for dusting

Place the sweet potatoes in a saucepan and cover with cold water. Cook for about 20 minutes, or until the potatoes are tender when pierced with a fork. Drain, peel, and mash the potatoes. Measure 1 cup of the puree and save any remaining puree for another use. Coat a soufflé dish with butter and dust lightly with flour.

Chop the orange zest finely. Combine with the potato puree. Sift together the flour, baking powder, baking soda, five-spice powder, and salt. Set aside.

With a mixer, beat together the eggs, oil, sugar, and buttermilk until just combined. Add the sweet potato mixture and beat until well mixed. Add the flour mixture and blend in well. The batter will be thick. Pour the batter into the prepared dish and place the dish in a steamer basket. Cover with a bamboo lid. Place the basket in a stainless-steel or coated-aluminum wok filled with enough water to reach 2 inches up the sides of the basket. Steam the cake for about 30 minutes, until a skewer inserted into the center comes out clean. Cool for 15 minutes. Dust with confectioners' sugar and serve warm.

Anise Cider Cranberry Rice Pudding

Rice pudding is one of my favorite desserts, but it's a guilty indulgence if made the conventional way. I came up with this version, which contains no dairy or eggs, yet is creamy, thanks to Asian sweet rice (also called sticky or glutinous rice).

SERVES 8

¾ cup apple cider
¼ cup cranberry juice
4 star anise pods
3 cinnamon sticks
6 whole cardamom pods
¾ cup sugar
½ cup long-grain white rice
¼ cup short-grain Asian sweet rice

In a small stainless-steel wok, combine the cider, cranberry juice, star anise, cinnamon sticks, and cardamom pods. Bring to a simmer, add the sugar, and stir to dissolve. Cover and remove from the heat. Let steep for 15 minutes, or until the cider mixture smells aromatic. Strain, and discard the spices.

In another stainless-steel or coated-aluminum wok, combine the two kinds of rice with 1½ cups of cold water. Over medium heat, bring to a boil and cook for 10 to 12 minutes, or until all the water is absorbed, but the rice is not dry. The rice will not be completely cooked. Stir in the cider mixture and cook for another 20 to 25 minutes, until the rice is creamy and the liquid is absorbed. Let the rice pudding cool. Serve warm or cold.

Jade Sea Pudding

This beautiful jade green pudding is a Hong Kong–style dessert that embodies the Chinese way with desserts in an up-to-date manner. The pudding, which is very soft—almost like a fruit soup—is served at the end of a meal. The beautiful green comes from honeydew melon—a popular flavor in Hong Kong. Different though this pudding is, I think you will enjoy it.

SERVES 8

⅔ cups pearl tapioca
2½ cups milk
2 slices peeled fresh ginger (each about the size of a quarter)
¼ teaspoon salt
3 tablespoons sugar
3 pounds honeydew melon
¼ teaspoon pure vanilla extract
¼ cup crystallized ginger, coarsely chopped, for garnish

Place the tapioca in a bowl and add cold water to cover. Place in the refrigerator and let the tapioca soak overnight. Drain. In a stainless-steel or coated-aluminum wok or saucepan, combine the tapioca, milk, ginger slices, and salt. Bring to a simmer and cook for 8 minutes, until the tapioca has swelled and almost all the milk is absorbed. Remove the ginger and discard. Add the sugar and stir to dissolve. Cool.

Cut the melon into chunks and place in the bowl of a food processor. Process into a fine puree. You should have 4 cups.

Add the melon puree and vanilla to the tapioca mixture and stir to blend. Spoon into individual glasses and chill. Top with crystallized ginger and serve.

Ginger Puffs

This simple variation on choux pastry makes a great dessert. Here the dough is flavored with ginger and then deep-fried in a wok. Mound the puffs and drizzle the flavored syrup over them, or keep the syrup thin and lay the puffs in a pool of sweetener. Either way, they are delicious!

MAKES 40 PUFFS

2 cups all-purpose flour, unsifted
½ teaspoon baking powder
1 cup milk
1 cup water
¼ teaspoon salt
6 tablespoons unsalted butter
⅓ cup finely slivered crystallized ginger
4 large eggs
2 cups oil
4 star anise pods
1 tablespoon finely slivered peeled fresh ginger
1 cup sugar

In a bowl, sift together the flour and baking powder. In a saucepan, combine the milk, water, salt, and butter. Bring to a boil, and add the flour mixture all at once, stirring with a wooden spoon until a ball of dough forms and pulls away from the sides of the saucepan. Keep stirring, and cook over low heat for about 5 minutes. Stir in the crystallized ginger, mixing it in well. Remove from the heat and cool. With a whisk or electric beater, add the eggs one at a time, whisking to incorporate well after each addition.

Pour the oil into a carbon-steel wok and heat to 350°F. over medium heat. With two wet teaspoons, form the dough into little balls and add to the hot oil. The dough will puff up and float to the top, turning a golden color. Remove with a slotted spoon and drain on paper towels.

Meanwhile, in a small saucepan, combine ⅓ cup of water with the star anise and slivered fresh ginger, and bring to a simmer over low heat. Add the sugar and stir to dissolve. Simmer for about 5 minutes, until the syrup thickens slightly and is flavorful. Remove from the heat and pour into a bowl. Let cool and strain before using.

Arrange the puffs on a serving platter or individual plates and serve with the flavored syrup.

Toffee Bananas

This popular dessert is often made with apples, but I chose bananas here. It is not only delicious but great fun, particularly for young children. The last step is a bit tricky, but it is one that your guests will have to take part in—since they create their own dessert. In order for the toffee on the bananas to harden, the water must stay icy cold, so be sure to have a good supply of ice on hand.

SERVES 6

3 ripe bananas
¼ cup cornstarch
¼ cup all-purpose flour
Pinch of salt
2 egg whites
1 cup (packed) dark brown sugar
¼ cup light corn syrup
¼ teaspoon fresh lemon juice
1 teaspoon Asian sesame oil
2 cups vegetable oil
A large bowl of ice water with ice cubes floating in it

Peel the bananas and cut into 2-inch segments. In a medium bowl, combine the cornstarch, flour, and salt. Stir in the egg whites and add enough water, about 2 tablespoons, to make a thin batter that will coat the bananas. Add the banana pieces to the batter.

In a small saucepan, combine the brown sugar, corn syrup, and lemon juice. Heat over low heat until the sugar is melted. Continue cooking until the syrup is light brown in color and a little drizzled onto a cold plate hardens. Immediately stand the saucepan in cold water to stop the cooking. Stir in the sesame oil with a wooden spoon. Cover and keep warm.

Heat the vegetable oil in a carbon-steel wok over medium-high heat until just smoking. Add the banana pieces and deep-fry to a golden brown. Remove with a slotted spoon and drain on paper towels. Mound the banana fritters on a warm plate and pour the warm syrup over them. Serve immediately with a bowl of ice-cold water set in the middle of the table. Each diner spears a banana fritter and dunks it in the ice water. The syrup will harden and form a crackling crust which breaks when eaten. The banana fritter should still be warm in the middle.

Peaches Poached in Gingered Wine

In the summer, when the fruit are in season and at the height of their flavor, make a large jar of these peaches. They keep well in the wine they have been cooked in, and are lovely to have on hand for a simple dessert, especially after an Asian meal. You can also use them on ice cream and pound cake, or with roasted and grilled meats; they are especially good with pork. Once the peaches have been eaten, you may reuse the wine to poach another batch, or even another kind of fruit.

SERVES 12

12 tree-ripened peaches
1 whole vanilla bean
1 bottle white port wine
1 tablespoon finely shredded peeled fresh ginger
5 whole green cardamom pods
1 cup sugar
2 cups water

Rinse the peaches in cold water and drain in a colander. With a sharp knife, cut the vanilla bean in half lengthwise.

In a stainless-steel or coated-aluminum wok, combine the port wine, vanilla bean, ginger, cardamom, sugar, and water. Over medium heat, bring the mixture to a boil, lower the heat, and simmer for about 5 minutes, or until the sugar is dissolved and the liquid is aromatic. Add the peaches and gently simmer until the fruit can be pricked easily with a skewer (see Note).

Remove the peaches with a slotted spoon; cool until they can be handled, and slip off the skins. Return the peeled peaches to the wine and cool completely. Cover and refrigerate overnight before serving. For longer storage, transfer the peaches and wine to a glass jar and keep in the refrigerator.

Note: The cooking time for the peaches depends on their ripeness. If they are underripe and hard, it can take as long as 45 minutes to 1 hour of poaching before they become tender. Ripe peaches will soften in 15 minutes.

Pears in Spiced Saffron Wine

Poaching pears in wine is a wonderful way to serve this fall fruit. The saffron gives the pears a lovely golden tinge and an exotic Eastern flavor. Often I use seckel pears when they are in season. If the pears are not ripe enough, don't be concerned—just poach them a little longer.

SERVES 6

2 lemons
6 ripe, firm pears
1 bottle of Champagne
1 cup white wine
¼ teaspoon saffron threads
2 teaspoons whole fenugreek
1 cup sugar
1 sheet parchment paper cut into a circle to fit inside the wok

Cut the lemons in half and squeeze them into a large bowl of cold water. Place the cut lemons in the water. Peel the pears and place them in the bowl of acidulated water, to prevent them from discoloring.

In a stainless-steel or coated-aluminum wok, combine the Champagne, white wine, saffron threads, fenugreek, and sugar. Bring to a boil, reduce the heat, and simmer, covered, for 10 minutes, or until the wine is flavored and the sugar dissolved. Add the pears to the liquid and cover with the parchment lid to keep them submerged. Return the liquid to a simmer and poach the pears for 20 to 30 minutes, or until they are tender and easily pierced with a skewer. Remove from the heat and cool in the wine. Serve immediately, or refrigerate the pears in their poaching liquid, well covered; they will keep for up to a month.

Note: For an easy sauce, remove the pears from the poaching liquid and reduce the liquid over high heat until syrupy; drizzle over the pears.

Candied Starfruits

When cut crosswise, this tropical fruit (also called carambola) naturally forms a star. Candied fruit is useful to have around to serve as a topping or just to eat out of hand. Starfruits prepared this way are also a very pretty garnish for ice cream, puddings, and cake. Look for ripe starfruit—fruits that are firm, yellow, and brown at the ridges.

MAKES 20 SLICES

4 starfruit
1½ cups water
1 cup sugar
6 whole star anise pods
1 teaspoon fennel seeds
6 cardamom pods
3 whole cloves

Wash the starfruits in cold water and dry thoroughly with paper towels. Trim away the brown ridges and cut crosswise into ¼-inch-thick slices.

In a stainless-steel or coated-aluminum wok, combine the water, sugar, star anise, fennel seeds, cardamom pods, and cloves. Bring to a boil, reduce the heat, and simmer, covered, for 10 minutes, or until the mixture is aromatic. Remove the cover and continue cooking the syrup for 15 to 20 minutes, or until it thickens enough just to coat the back of a wooden spoon. Add the starfruits and cook for 3 to 5 minutes, or just until they are tender. With a slotted spoon, remove them to a plate. Cook the liquid for about 30 minutes over high heat until it is thick and syrupy. Cool to tepid, then pour over the starfruits and let stand until completely cool. If not using immediately, transfer to a glass jar and store, covered, in the refrigerator; the candied fruits will keep for several weeks.

resources

Asian Ingredients

Adriana's Caravan
409 Vanderbilt Street
Brooklyn, NY 11218
(800) 316-0820 or
   (718) 436-8565
email: adricara@aol.com
www.adrianascaravan.com
Spices and condiments

Chinese American
   Trading Co. Inc.
91 Mulberry Street
New York, NY 10013
(212) 267-5224
fax: (212) 619-7446
Spices and dried foods

EthnicGrocer.com
*Asian condiments, oils, and
   dry goods*

Kam Man Food Products
200 Canal Street
New York, NY 10013
(212) 571-0330
*Chinese and Japanese
   products*

Spice Merchant
4125 South Highway 89
P.O. Box 524
Jackson Hole, WY 83001
(800) 551-5999
fax: (307) 733-6343
*Asian ingredients, equip-
ment, and dishes.*

Uwajimaya
519 6th Avenue, South
Seattle, WA 98104
(800) 889-1928
fax: (206) 624-6915
Uwajimaya.com
Japanese products

Seed Sources

The Cook's Garden
P.O. Box 535
Londonderry, VT 85148
(802) 824-3400
fax: (802) 824-3027

Shepherd's Garden Seeds
30 Irene Street
Torrington, CT 06790
(203) 482-3638
www.shepherdseeds.com

bibliography

Bissenden, Rosemary. *Asia's Undiscovered Cuisine.* New York: Pantheon, 1970.
Fukahasa, Hiroho, and Yasuko Takahasa. *Healthy Japanese Cooking.* New York: Weatherhill, Inc., 1979.
Ju Lin, Hsiang, and Tsu Feng Liu. *Chinese Gastronomy.* New York: Harvest, 1977.
McDermott, Nancy. *Real Thai.* San Francisco: Chronicle, 1992.

index

conversion chart
Equivalent Imperial and Metric Measurements

American cooks use standard containers, the 8-ounce cup and a tablespoon that takes exactly 16 level fillings to fill that cup level. Measuring by cup makes it very difficult to give weight equivalents, as a cup of densely packed butter will weigh considerably more than a cup of flour. The easiest way therefore to deal with cup measurements in recipes is to take the amount by volume rather than by weight. Thus the equation reads:

1 cup = 240 ml = 8 fl. oz. ½ cup = 120 ml = 4 fl. oz.

It is possible to buy a set of American cup measures in major stores around the world.

In the States, butter is often measured in sticks. One stick is the equivalent of 8 tablespoons. One tablespoon of butter is therefore the equivalent to ½ ounce or 15 grams.

LIQUID MEASURES

Fluid Ounces	U.S.	Imperial	Milliliters
	1 teaspoon	1 teaspoon	5
¼	2 teaspoons	1 dessertspoon	10
½	1 tablespoon	1 tablespoon	14
1	2 tablespoons	2 tablespoons	28
2	¼ cup	4 tablespoons	56
4	½ cup		110
5		¼ pint or 1 gill	140
6	¾ cup		170
8	1 cup		225
9			250, ¼ liter
10	1¼ cups	½ pint	280
12	1½ cups		340
15		¾ pint	420
16	2 cups		450
18	2¼ cups		500, ½ liter
20	2½ cups	1 pint	560
24	3 cups		675
25		1¼ pints	700
27	3½ cups		750
30	3¾ cups	1½ pints	840
32	4 cups or 1 quart		900
35		1¾ pints	980
36	4½ cups		1000, 1 liter
40	5 cups	2 pints or 1 quart	1120

SOLID MEASURES

U.S. and Imperial Measures		Metric Measures	
Ounces	Pounds	Grams	Kilos
1		28	
2		56	
3½		100	
4	¼	112	
5		140	
6		168	
8	½	225	
9		250	¼
12	¾	340	
16	1	450	
18		500	½
20	1¼	560	
24	1½	675	
27		750	¾
28	1¾	780	
32	2	900	
36	2¼	1000	1
40	2½	1100	
48	3	1350	
54		1500	1½

OVEN TEMPERATURE EQUIVALENTS

Fahrenheit	Celsius	Gas Mark	Description
225	110	¼	Cool
250	130	½	
275	140	1	Very Slow
300	150	2	
325	170	3	Slow
350	180	4	Moderate
375	190	5	
400	200	6	Moderately Hot
425	220	7	Fairly Hot
450	230	8	Hot
475	240	9	Very Hot
500	250	10	Extremely Hot

Any broiling recipes can be used with the grill of the oven, but beware of high-temperature grills.

EQUIVALENTS FOR INGREDIENTS

all-purpose flour—plain flour
baking sheet—oven tray
buttermilk—ordinary milk
cheesecloth—muslin
coarse salt—kitchen salt
cornstarch—cornflour

eggplant—aubergine
granulated sugar—caster sugar
half and half—12% fat milk
heavy cream—double cream
light cream—single cream
parchment paper—greaseproof paper

plastic wrap—cling film
scallion—spring onion
shortening—white fat
unbleached flour—strong, white flour
zest—rind
zucchini—courgettes or marrow